NAPOLEON HILL'S
IMAGINE IT, ACHIEVE IT

NAPOLEON HILL BOOKS BY THE NAPOLEON HILL FOUNDATION

Think and Grow Rich

Lessons on Success

A Lifetime of Riches

Freedom from Your Fears

A Treasury of Success—Unlimited

Andrew Carnegie's Mental Dynamite

Napoleon Hill's Speak It Into Reality

Napoleon Hill's Imagine It, Achieve It

Master Mind—The Memoirs of Napoleon Hill

Napoleon Hill's Guide to Achieving Your Goals

Napoleon Hill's First Editions on Mastering Personal and Professional Success

NAPOLEON HILL'S
IMAGINE IT, ACHIEVE IT

SHAPE YOUR FUTURE BY TURNING YOUR THOUGHTS INTO ACTION

AN OFFICIAL PUBLICATION OF THE
NAPOLEON HILL FOUNDATION

© Copyright 2025– The Napoleon Hill Foundation

All rights reserved. This book is protected by the copyright laws of the United States of America. No part of this publication may be reproduced, stored in or introduced into a retrieval system, or transmitted, in any form or by any means (electronic, mechanical, photocopying, recording or otherwise), without the prior written permission of the publisher. For permissions requests, contact the publisher, addressed "Attention: Permissions Coordinator," at the address below.

Published and distributed by:

SOUND WISDOM
P.O. Box 310
Shippensburg, PA 17257-0310

717-530-2122

info@soundwisdom.com

www.soundwisdom.com

While efforts have been made to verify information contained in this publication, neither the author nor the publisher assumes any responsibility for errors, inaccuracies, or omissions. While this publication is chock-full of useful, practical information; it is not intended to be legal or accounting advice. All readers are advised to seek competent lawyers and accountants to follow laws and regulations that may apply to specific situations. The reader of this publication assumes responsibility for the use of the information. The author and publisher assume no responsibility or liability whatsoever on the behalf of the reader of this publication.

The scanning, uploading and distribution of this publication via the Internet or via any other means without the permission of the publisher is illegal and punishable by law. Please purchase only authorized editions and do not participate in or encourage piracy of copyrightable materials.

ISBN 13 TP: 978-1-64095-634-6

ISBN 13 eBook: 978-1-64095-635-3

For Worldwide Distribution, Printed in the U.S.A.

1 2 3 4 5 6 7 8 / 29 28 27 26 25

CONTENTS

	Introduction 7
Chapter 1	Mind Control 11
Chapter 2	Redesign Your Imaginations Into Reality.... 21
Chapter 3	Master of Your Own Fate................. 37
Chapter 4	Purpose Is Personal Power 49
Chapter 5	Engaging Your Emotions 61
Chapter 6	Facing and Overcoming Fear.............. 77
Chapter 7	Imagining Ideals........................ 93
Chapter 8	Motivations and Machinations........... 107
Chapter 9	Rhythm of Thought 121
Chapter 10	Freestyle Freedoms..................... 131
	Conclusion 145
	About Napoleon Hill................... 151

INTRODUCTION

NAPOLEON HILL is the author of *Think and Grow Rich* (over 100 million copies sold!), *Master Key to Riches,* and other best-selling books. He is also the creator of the American Philosophy of Individual Achievement. His discussion on "going the extra mile" has made hundreds of thousands of wealthy men and women worldwide who have taken the time to put his wisdom into practice in their lives.

Every person needs a philosophy of life, and in Dr. Hill's books you will find the principles to guide you and sustain you in whatever work you have chosen. His philosophy does not conflict in any way with your religion or your political beliefs—but rather augments and amplifies them.

Although written a few decades ago, the wisdom, advice, humor, and proven-successful strategies are just as relevant now than they were then—in fact, even more so.

Image It, Achieve It shares powerful and successful approaches to living your best life. This mini but mighty book is inspired by Napoleon Hill's timeless principles for personal victory and career accomplishment. Learn how your imaginations—the thoughts your mind creates—can redesign your reality, your fate, and your purpose to achieve your greatest goals.

This book dives into how daydreams, ruminations, and even fantasies can shape your daily routines as well as long-term plans. *Imagine It, Achieve It* also delves into the importance of your tamest and even wildest imaginations! You will learn how to:

- Create substantive ideas out of impulses.
- Develop concrete concepts from moments of fantasy.
- Leverage emotions to amplify your desires.
- Overcome negativity with positivity.

Whether striving to achieve financial success, personal growth, or spiritual fulfillment, this book provides the tools to transform your mindset and speak your dreams into existence. You can start changing your reality today—one imagination at a time.

INTRODUCTION

We at the Napoleon Hill Foundation hope this mini-book will inspire you to look into Napoleon Hill's original books that delve more deeply into matters of personal achievement, helping you reach that point in life when all of your plans have been fulfilled and you achieve every goal.

Don M. Green
Chief Executive Officer and Executive Director
Napoleon Hill Foundation

CHAPTER 1

MIND CONTROL

Whatever the mind can conceive
and believe, the mind can achieve!

Y OUR IMAGINATIONS, the thoughts in your mind, hold the power to transform your greatest desires into their material counterparts. Your efforts to achieve success can either be hindered or accelerated based on your understanding of the language of thought—your imaginations. By gaining fluency in this language, you can enlarge your capacity for personal achievement and enjoy the fruits of peace of mind, improved interpersonal relationships, and reaching career goals.

When you study and apply the wisdom contained in this book, you will maximize the ability of your imaginations, ideas, and thoughts to generate lasting change in your world—at home, with friends, in your work environment. You can easily translate theory into practice—into *action*.

There is something about the power of thought that seems to attract to a person the material equivalent of their aims and purposes. This power is not man-made. But it was made for mankind to use, and to enable individuals to control much of their earthly destiny.

The single most powerful tool available to human beings is not money, physical strength, influence, or a network—it is your mind. Your thoughts determine your outcomes in life, as well as your experience of the journey. Thought is the only power that can systematically organize, accumulate, and assemble facts and materials according to a definite plan. Whether you succeed in your personal and professional life, and whether you can recognize and appreciate your success, is dependent on the nature of your thoughts.

Thankfully, our thoughts are the sole element in our lives that are completely within our control. Regardless of external circumstances—no matter the environment we are born into or in where we currently find ourselves—we can use our thoughts to translate our desires into reality.

You will attract to you the very things, or the very station in life, that you create in your thoughts. To harness your thoughts to create material success, you do not require any personal advantage such as wealth, connections, or education. You simply need to leverage the mental resources already within your possession by cultivating a thorough understanding of the workings of the mind and how thoughts may be transformed into their physical counterparts.

You can use your imaginations to translate your desires into reality.

The mind is the control station for our existence. It filters the infinite number of sensations that bombard our receptive organs, rearranges, combines, and stores a percentage of these impressions, and draws on memories and active thought impulses to guide our actions and reactions.

All our mental and behavioral habits originate from the matter of thought, our imaginations. Thoughts and ideas are intangible, yet physical in nature. And because thought is matter—energy that signals to our bodies, our surroundings, and other bodies in proximity to us—it can be manipulated to create palpable results in the physical environment.

Not only do our thoughts produce real effects in nature, but they also transform our character and personality. We come to resemble the nature of our dominating thoughts.

Our personality will be magnetic, positive, and attractive if the mind is free of negative thoughts and emotions. Our personality will be negative, alienating, and self-centered if our thoughts are characterized by fear and negativity. We are, therefore, the architects of our character and our life and must plan and assemble our thoughts as we would a house.

> **Your thoughts transform your character and personality to resemble the nature of your dominating thoughts. Your personality is magnetic, positive, and attractive if your mind is free of negative thoughts and emotions.**

But first we need to understand how thoughts work together as building units, and we need a blueprint to guide us toward arranging the units to fashion a solid mental framework. We need to become fluent in the language of thought.

As psychoanalysts found in the nineteenth century, the mind has its own language—a language that can be decoded to understand our subconscious fears and desires, yes, but also a language that can be restructured and enhanced to improve our mental and behavioral habits.

In order to get what we want in life, we have to learn to think more efficiently, more purposefully, and more programmatically. Only when our thoughts are conditioned to be active, definite, and accurate can we attract opportunities and riches into our life, as well as become more resilient to temporary defeat.

When we learn to govern the workings of our own mind, it becomes easy to build influence, garner support, and attract opportunities. As Rosa Lee Hill writes, "People actually pick up our thoughts, our state of mind, and reflect these thoughts right back to us in both attitude and spoken words."[1] There is nothing more powerful than a self-disciplined, controlled mind—except one that is given free rein to imagine the unimaginable.

The following chapters provide a guide for generating more powerful thoughts so you can live and work with more intention, joy, and success. When you learn to maximize your thoughts and habits, you will attract the positive workings of

---

1. Rosa Lee Hill and Napoleon Hill, *How to Attract Men and Money* (Sound Wisdom, 2021), 77.

the universal law of nature that turns impulses into habits and habits into rhythms, which give you increased momentum on your success journey.

You will no longer be held back by fears, doubts, and difficulties, nor will the lures of procrastination and indecision thwart your progress. *Everything will feel in sync and meaningful, like you are doing exactly what you are meant to be doing—and succeeding at it.* Even when challenges come—and they will—you will thrive because you will see these not as setbacks but rather as opportunities in disguise. There are no limitations to the mind conditioned for success.

> **More than a philosophical concept— it's a practical, life-changing method of imagining and achieving.**

You are doing much more than reading a philosophy of the mind; you are starting a life-changing method of mental discipline. Too many success concepts emphasize self-control as the key to individual achievement; however, self-control is merely the control over actions and words exhibited after already losing control of your mind. Mental discipline, in contrast, involves controlling your thoughts so that your actions and words are disposed for success.

Mind control uproots negative thoughts and plants constructive impulses in their place, growing a fertile field of positive thoughts that seek outlet in definite plans of action. Gaining fluency in the language of the mind is the first step to disciplining your thoughts—the second is applying what you learn by speaking the language. The third is balancing discipline and the freedom to imagine.

You are living in the most advantageous age in the entire history of the world, and regardless of what your present station in life may be or how humble your beginning, the possibilities ahead of you may stagger your imagination—which is good. You are living in an age that affords every needed stimulant to arouse your imagination and inspire you with ambition.

Great fortune begins with great imagination.

The story of practically every great fortune starts with the day when a creator of ideas and a seller of ideas got together and worked in harmony. Andrew Carnegie, one of the wealthiest businessmen of the 19th century, surrounded himself with people who could do what he could not do, people who imagined. They created ideas and put those ideas into operation—and that made him and others fabulously rich.

Millions of people go through life hoping for favorable "breaks." Perhaps a favorable break can get you an opportunity, but the safest plan is not to depend on luck. It was a favorable "break" that gave me the biggest opportunity of my life—but more than twenty years of determined effort was devoted to that opportunity before it became an asset.

The break consisted of my good fortune in meeting and gaining the cooperation of Andrew Carnegie. Carnegie planted in my mind the idea of organizing the principles of achievement into a philosophy of success. Millions of people have profited by the discoveries made in the years of research, and fortunes have been accumulated through the application of the philosophy. The beginning was simple. It was an idea that anyone might have imagined and developed.

The favorable break came through Carnegie, but what about the determination, definiteness of purpose, and the desire to attain the goal, and the persistent effort of all those years of research? It was no ordinary desire that survived disappointment, discouragement, temporary defeat, criticism, and the constant reminding that I was wasting my time. It was a burning desire! An obsession!

When the idea was first planted in my mind by Mr. Carnegie, it was coaxed, nursed, and enticed to remain alive. Gradually, the idea became a giant under its own power, and it drove me each day. Ideas are like that. First you give life and action and guidance to imagination, then they take on a power of their own and sweep aside all opposition.

Imaginative ideas are intangible forces, but they have more power than the physical brains that give birth to them. They have the power to live on, after the brain that creates them has returned to dust.

I urge you to climb aboard a force that is practically irresistible—a force that will carry you on to the very summit of achievement of the highest order—if you will make it your business and your life work to control and use your mind and its full potential to help make the world a better place for you, your family, your neighborhood, and your nation.

☞ Questions to Consider

- How in control are you of your mind—your fears, thoughts, and desires—as you move through your daily life?

- Is your mind under your control or do you allow negative and unhealthy thoughts to intrude throughout your day?

- Imagine you are building a house in your mind. What building materials would you use? What would you avoid using?

CHAPTER 2

REDESIGN YOUR IMAGINATIONS INTO REALITY

The imagination is the workshop of the soul where all the plans for individual achievement are shaped.

THE IMAGINATION is literally the workshop where all plans are created. It is where the impulse, the desire, is given shape, form, and action through the imaginative faculty of the mind.

We can create anything we can imagine.

Through imagination we have discovered and effectively channeled more of nature's forces during the past 50 years than during the entire history of the human race previous to that time. And even with all we have accomplished, we have come nowhere near the limit of what we are capable.

TWO FORMS OF IMAGINATION

Our mind's imaginative faculty functions in two forms: synthetic imagination and creative imagination. Let's look at each in more detail.

Synthesized imagination means you arrange old concepts, ideas, or plans into new combinations. Synthesized imagination does not *create* anything. It merely works with the material of experience, education, and observation that it is fed. It is the faculty used by most inventors, with the exception of those geniuses who draw upon the creative imagination when they cannot solve problems through synthesized imagination.

Creative imagination is the faculty that the finite human mind has direct communication with Infinite Intelligence, where hunches and inspirations are received. This is where all basic or new ideas are handed over to humankind. Through creative imagination we pick up "vibes" from other people; and in that way, one individual may tune in or communicate with the subconscious minds of others.

The creative imagination works automatically, but only when your conscious mind is motivated, energized, and working at such a high rate that it becomes very perceptive and receptive, such as when the conscious mind is stimulated through the emotion of a strong desire.

Great leaders of business, industry, and finance, and the great artists, musicians, poets, and writers became great because they developed the faculty of creative imagination.

Desire is a thought, an impulse. It is nebulous and ephemeral. It is abstract and of no value until it has been transformed into its physical counterpart. While the synthesized imagination is used most frequently in the process of transforming desire into money, there are circumstances and situations that demand the use of the creative imagination as well.

Note: For example, it's safe to say that all of the innovations in internet services—social media, eCommerce, music/video/movie site, news sites, etc.—are combinations of these two imaginations working overtime in the minds of the inventors.

Your imagination becomes more receptive in direct response to how often you use it.

Both the synthesized and the creative imagination become more alert and receptive with use. And though your imaginative faculty may have become weak through lack of use, you can revive it. Just as any muscle or organ of the body develops the more it is used, your imagination also becomes more receptive in direct response to the amount that you use it.

USE YOUR SYNTHESIZED IMAGINATION

First let's focus on the development of the synthesized imagination that you use most often in converting desire into achieving your goals.

Transformation of the intangible impulse of desire into the tangible reality of, let's say money, calls for a plan, or plans. To make plans you must use your imagination. Mainly this requires you to use your synthesized imagination as you draw on your experience, education, and observations.

An excellent example of synthesized imagination is Thomas Edison's invention of the light bulb. He began with one recognized fact that other people had discovered: a wire could be heated by electricity until it produced light. The problem was that the intense heat quickly burned the wire out and the light never lasted more than a few minutes.

Most so-called failures are only temporary defeats.

Edison failed more than ten thousand times in his attempt to control this heat. When he found the method, it was by applying another common fact that had simply eluded everyone else. He realized that charcoal is produced by setting wood on fire, covering it with soil, and allowing the fires to smolder. The soil permits only enough air to reach the fire to keep it burning without blazing, and that way the wood isn't burned up.

When Edison recognized this fact, his imagination immediately associated it with the idea of heating the wire. He placed the wire inside a bottle, pumped out most of the air, and produced the first incandescent light. It burned for eight-and-a-half hours.

Everything that Edison used to make the electric light was widely known, but the way he synthesized the knowledge changed the world. And made him a very wealthy man.

W. Clement Stone called the process the R2A2 formula—Recognize and Relate, Assimilate and Apply. If you do that with everything you see, hear, think, and experience it will give you a new way of looking at familiar things. If you do that, you can achieve what others believe is impossible.

TAPPING INTO
CREATIVE IMAGINATION

As far as science has been able to determine, the entire universe consists of four things—time, space, matter, and energy. Moreover, and this statement is of stupendous importance—this earth, every one of the billions of individual cells of your body, and every subatomic particle of matter, began as an intangible form of energy. Through the combination of energy and matter everything perceptible has been created, from the largest star in the heavens down to and including human beings.

Desire is a thought impulse that are forms of energy. When you begin the process of acquiring money by using the thought impulse of desire, you are drafting into your service the same "stuff" that nature used in creating this earth, as well as every material form in the universe, including your body and brain where the imaginative thought impulses function.

You are engaged in trying to turn your desire into its physical or monetary counterpart, and there are laws of physics and principles of psychology that can help you. But first you must give yourself time to become familiar with these laws, and learn to use them. Through repetition, and by describing these principles from every conceivable angle, I hope to reveal to you the secret through which every great fortune has been accumulated.

Strange and paradoxical as it may seem, the "secret" is not a secret. It is made obvious in the earth, the stars, the planets, in the elements above and around us, in every blade of grass, and every form of life within our vision.

Don't be discouraged if you don't fully understand or accept this theory. I don't expect that you will accept all that is in this book on your first reading. Assimilate as much as you can now as you read this for the first time. Later, when you reread and study it, you will discover that something has happened to clarify it and give you a broader understanding of the whole. Above all, don't stop nor hesitate in your study of these principles until you have read the book at least three times. Then, you will not want to stop.

PRACTICAL USE OF IMAGINATION

Ideas are the beginning points of all fortunes and the products of the imagination. The following are two true stories about ideas that have yielded huge fortunes. These stories convey how important imagination can play in turning an idea into success. They illustrate the method imagination can be used in accumulating riches.

The Enchanted Kettle

In the late 1880s, an old country doctor drove to town, hitched his horse, quietly slipped into a drug store by the back door, and began bartering with the young drug clerk.

For more than an hour, behind the prescription counter, the old doctor and the clerk talked in low tones. Then the doctor left. He went out to the buggy and brought back a large, old-fashioned kettle, a big wooden paddle to stir the contents of the kettle, and deposited them at the back of the store.

The clerk inspected the kettle, reached into his inside pocket, took out a roll of bills, and handed it to the doctor. The roll contained exactly five hundred dollars—the clerk's entire savings!

The doctor handed over a small slip of paper on which was written a secret formula. The words on that small slip of paper were worth a king's ransom. But not to the doctor. Those magic words were needed to start the kettle to boiling, but neither the doctor nor the young clerk knew what fabulous fortunes were destined to flow from that kettle.

The old doctor was glad to sell the outfit for five hundred dollars. The clerk was taking a big chance by staking his entire life's savings on a mere scrap of paper and an old kettle. He never dreamed his investment would start a kettle to overflowing with gold that would one day surpass the miraculous performance of Aladdin's lamp.

What the clerk really purchased was an idea!

The old kettle and the wooden paddle and the secret message on a slip of paper, were incidental. The miracle of that kettle only began to take place after the new owner mixed with the secret instructions an ingredient the doctor knew nothing about.

See if you can discover what it was that the young man added to the secret message that caused the kettle to overflow with gold. Here you have a story of facts stranger than fiction—facts that began in the form of an idea.

Just look at the vast fortunes of gold this idea has produced. It has paid and still pays huge fortunes to people worldwide who distribute the contents of the kettle to millions of people.

The old kettle is now one of the world's largest consumers of sugar, thus providing jobs to thousands of people engaged in growing sugar cane, and in refining and marketing sugar.

The old kettle consumes, annually, millions of glass and plastic bottles and cans, providing jobs to huge numbers of workers.

The old kettle provides employment to an army of clerks, copywriters, and advertising experts throughout the nation. It has brought fame and fortune to scores of artists who have created magnificent pictures describing the product.

The old kettle has converted Atlanta, which was a small southern city, into the business capital of the South, where it now benefits, directly or indirectly, every business and practically every resident of the city.

The influence of this idea now benefits every civilized country in the world, pouring out a continuous stream of gold to all who touch it. Gold from the kettle built and maintains one of the most prominent colleges of the South, where thousands of young people receive training essential for success.

If the product of that old brass kettle could talk, it would tell thrilling tales in every language. Tales of love, business, professional men and women who are daily being stimulated by it.

I am sure of at least one such tale of romance, for I was part of it, and it all began not far from the very spot on which the drug clerk purchased the old kettle. There is where I met my wife, and it was she who first told me of the enchanted kettle. It was the product of that kettle we were drinking when I asked her to accept me "for better or worse."

Whoever you are, wherever you may live, whatever your occupation, just remember every time you see the words Coca-Cola, that its vast empire of wealth and influence grew out of a single idea. And that idea, the mysterious ingredient the drug clerk—Asa Candler—mixed with the secret formula was... imagination!

Stop and think of that for a moment.

Keep in mind that the steps to riches described in this book are the very same principles through which the influence of Coca-Cola has been extended to every city, town, village, and crossroads of the of the world. Now here's the most important thing to remember—the ideas you create from your imagination may have the possibility of duplicating the enormous success of this worldwide thirst-killer.

TRANSMUTING IDEAS INTO CASH

Asa Candler knew the astounding truth that ideas can be transmuted into cash through the power of definite purpose, plus definite plans.

If you believe that hard work and honesty alone will bring riches, you can forget it! It is not true. Riches, when they come in huge quantities, are never the result of hard work alone. Riches come, if they come at all, in response to definite demands based on the application of definite principles, and not by chance or luck.

Generally speaking, an idea is a thought that prompts you to action because it appeals to your imagination. All master salespeople know that ideas can be sold where merchandise cannot. Ordinary salespeople do not know this. That is why they are "ordinary."

A publisher of low-priced books made a discovery that has been worth much to publishers. He learned that many people buy titles, not the contents of books. By merely changing the name of one book that was not moving, his sales of that book jumped upward more than a million copies. The inside of the book was not changed in any way. He merely ripped off the cover and put on a new cover with a title that had "box-office" appeal.

That, as simple as it may seem, was an idea—someone imagined it.

> The Post-it Note may have been a godsend, literally. In the early 1970s, Arthur Fry was in search of a bookmark for his church hymnal that would neither fall out nor damage the hymnal. Fry noticed that a colleague at 3M, Dr. Spencer Silver, had developed an adhesive in 1968 that was strong enough to stick to surfaces, but left no residue after removal and could be repositioned. Fry took some of Silver's adhesive and applied it along the edge of a piece of paper. His church hymnal problem was solved.
>
> Fry soon realized that his "bookmark" had other potential functions when he used it to leave a note on a work file, and coworkers kept dropping by, seeking "bookmarks" for their offices. This "bookmark" was a new way to communicate and to organize. 3M Corporation crafted the name Post-it Note for Arthur Fry's new bookmarks and began production in the late 1970s for commercial use.
>
> In 1977, test markets failed to show consumer interest. However in 1979, 3M implemented a massive consumer sampling strategy, and the Post-it Note took off. Today, we see the Post-it

Notes peppered across files, computers, desks, and doors in offices and homes throughout the country. From a church hymnal bookmark to an office and home essential, the Post-it Note has colored the way we work.

In 2003, 3M came out with "Post-It Brand Super Sticky Notes," with a stronger glue that adheres better to vertical and non-smooth surfaces.

Arthur Fry was born in Minnesota. As a child, he showed signs of being an inventor making his own toboggans from scraps of wood. Fry attended the University of Minnesota where he studied Chemical Engineering. While still a student in 1953, Fry began working for 3M in the New Product Development he stayed with 3M his entire working life.

Spencer Silver was born in San Antonio. In 1962, he received his bachelor of science degree in chemistry from Arizona State University. In 1966, he received his PhD in organic chemistry from the University of Colorado. In 1967, he became a senior chemist for 3M's Central Research Labs specializing in adhesives technology. Silver is also an accomplished painter. He has received more than 20 U.S. patents.[2]

---

2. Mary Bellis, "Invention of the Post-it Note," October 16, 2019, *ThoughtCo.;* https://www.thoughtco.com/history-of-post-it-note-1992326; accessed April 9, 2025.

There is no standard price on ideas. The creator of ideas sets his or her own price, and, if they are smart, they get it.

The only limitations are those we set up in our own minds.

👉 Questions to Consider

- Do you most often use your *synthesized imagination*—arranging old concepts, ideas, or plans into new combinations? Or *creative imagination*—directly communicating with Infinite Intelligence, receiving hunches and inspirations are received?

- Have you picked up "vibes" from other people, tuning in or communicating with the subconscious minds of others?

- Do you still believe that hard work and honesty will bring you riches?

- What do you think of the "Enchanted Kettle" story? Is there such a kettle in your position?

CHAPTER 3

MASTER OF YOUR OWN FATE

Self-discipline closes the door against jealousy, hatred, revenge, greed, anger and superstition, and opens the door to friendship, goodwill, confidence and love.

O F THE UTMOST SIGNIFICANCE is the fact that the Creator provided humankind with the one and only means by which we have broken away from the animal family and ascended into spiritual estates, where we may be the master of our own earthly fate.

The means provided is the law of change. By the simple process of changing your mental attitude, you can draw any pattern of life and live as you choose and make that pattern a reality. This is the one and only aspect of life over which you have been provided with irrevocable, unchallenged, and unchallengeable powers of absolute control. A fact which suggests that it must have been considered by the Creator to be the most important prerogative of humanity.

> **You have absolute control over your mental attitude.**

Dictators and would-be world conquerors come and go. They always *go* because it is not part of the overall plan of the universe for us to be enslaved. It is rather part of the eternal pattern that every person shall be free, to live their own lives their own way, to control their thoughts and deeds, to make their own earthly destiny.

That is why the philosopher who looks backward into the past to determine what is going to happen in the yet unborn future, cannot get excited because a Hitler or a Stalin momentarily basks in the light of his own ego and threatens the freedom of mankind. For these men, like all others of their ilk who have preceded them, will destroy themselves with their own excesses and vanities and their lusts for power over the free world. Moreover, these would-be stranglers of human freedom may be only demons who unwittingly serve as shock troops to awaken humanity from complacency and make way for the change that will bring new and better ways of living.

Nature leads us through change after change by peaceful means as long as we cooperate, but resorts to revolutionary methods if we rebel and neglect or refuse to conform to the law of change. The revolutionary method may consist of the death of a loved one or a severe illness; it may bring a failure in business, or the loss of a job, which forces people to change their occupation and seek employment in an entirely new field, where they find greater opportunities never known if old habits had not been broken up.

Nature enforces the law of fixation of habits in every living thing lower than humans, and just as definitely enforces the law of change in our habits. Nature thus provides the only means by which we may grow and evolve in accordance with our fixed position in the overall plan of the universe.

For example, Thomas A. Edison's first major adversity was experienced when his teacher sent him home after only three months in an elementary grade school, with a note to his parents saying he did not have the capacity to be educated. He never went back to school—a conventional school, that is—but he began to school himself in the great University of Hard

Knocks, where he gained an education that made him one of the greatest inventors of all times.

Before Edison was graduated from that university, he was fired from one job after another, while the hand of destiny guided him through the *essential changes* that prepared him to grow and evolve into becoming a great inventor. Formal schooling, perhaps, would have spoiled his chances of becoming great.

Always look for healing, happiness, success, victory, and move forward.

When adversity, physical pain, sorrow, distress, failure and temporary defeat try to stop you in your tracks, instead of crying out in rebellion or shivering with fear, hold your head high and look in all directions for the seed of an equivalent benefit that is carried in every circumstance of adversity. Look for healing, happiness, joy, success, and move forward.

Most likely you have heard the term "tough love." It is a technique wherein reality encounters fantasy head-on and is intended to jerk the recipient back to the here and now for their own good. When parents apply this practice, it frequently involves saying "no" or withholding some requested item such as money, a car, a down payment, or anything that the son or daughter is requesting that, in the minds of the parents, will not contribute in a positive way to the general good of the child.

Children grow up, parents die, and soon we realize that we are in their position and sometimes find ourselves saying "no" to our own inner child. Maturity comes about through positive growth and frequently each of us can get in our own way. When we reach a developmental crossroads, we often prefer to take the traditional path and not put ourselves through extra work.

Saying "yes" to the mundane can have its consequences too, because sooner rather than later we find that our path does not lead to growth but to stagnation. The antidote to this illness of attitude is called self-discipline—the ultimate way of being the ruler of your own fate.

CLOSE THE DOOR

Each person is gifted with a conscience that generally works pretty well and provides good advice, if we use it. Still, we often allow ourselves to linger in regret over past occurrences, mistakes, losses, and the like rather than positioning ourselves face forward toward a better future.

For example, by closing the door tightly on your past and not lingering in the threshold, you can move forward toward your life's purpose. This is not to say that you become hard-hearted or without compassion, but rather that you apply tough love to yourself and care about who you are as much as you care about others.

Today, ask yourself if there is a door you have left ajar. Are you afraid to slam it shut and lock it and throw away the key? Consider that this option for retreat could be the reason you are not moving forward. You are allowing a former setback to prevent your glorious comeback. Close that door now, and linger no further. New doors await you, and when you knock the doors will open and lead you to your destiny. Why wait? Make all things new.

Self-Made Patterns

These times can be viewed optimistically or pessimistically depending on the mindset you create. Good always exists within the bad, and vice versa. Training yourself to focus on the good enables you to recognize the good when it presents itself in your life. Likewise, focusing on the bad attracts more of the same to you because you have set up an antenna for it. Thoughts migrate just like birds and fish. There is an instinctual homing device that directs their movements. Unlike creatures that are programmed by instinct, we humans create our own patterns.

You can create your own patterns, habits, and choices in life.

What patterns are you designing for your life? You *do* have the power to choose. Choose wisely and on purpose.

Consider the rather serious problems that arise in your mind in connection with disappointments and failures of the past, and the broken hearts that occur as the result of the loss of material things or the loss of friends or loved ones.

Self-control or self-discipline is the only real solution for such problems. It begins with recognizing the fact that there are only two kinds of problems—those you can solve, and those you can't solve.

The problem that can be solved should immediately be cleared by the most practical means available—and those that have no solution should be put out of your mind and forgotten.

Let's think, for a minute, about this process of forgetting. Refer to it as closing the door on some unpleasantness that is disturbing your emotional equilibrium. Mastery over all emotions, can enable you to close the door between yourself and the unpleasant experience of the past. You must close the door tightly and lock it securely, so that there is no possibility of its being opened again.

This is the way to treat unsolvable problems, too. Those who lack self-discipline often stand in the doorway and look wistfully backward into the past, instead of closing the door and looking forward into the future.

This door closing is a valuable technique. It requires the support of a good, strong will, and you have a strong will if you have the departments of your mind organized and under the control of your ego, as they should be.

Door closing does not make you hard, cold, or unemotional, but it does require firmness. Self-control cannot permit lurking memories of sad experiences, and it wastes no time worrying over problems that have no solution. You cannot yield to the temptation to relive your unhappy memories, for they destroy your creative force, undermine your initiative, weaken your imagination, disturb your faculty of reason, and generally confuse the departments of your mind.

The Power of Your Will

You must place the power of your will against the door that shuts out what you wish to forget, or you do not acquire self-discipline. Self-control closes the door tightly against all manner of fears, and opens wide the doors of hope and faith!

Self-discipline closes the door against jealousy, hatred, revenge, greed, anger, and superstition, and opens the door to joy, friendship, goodwill, confidence, and love.

Self-control closes the door tightly against all manner of fears, and opens wide the doors of hope and faith!

Self-discipline looks forward, not backward. It roots out discouragement and worry and other negative emotions. And it not only encourages positive emotions, it forces them to come before the faculty of reason every time they express themselves so that they, too, may be kept under control.

Disciplining yourself makes your mind strong. It enables you to take possession of your mind and exercise your God-given right to control your mental attitude. You do not have real self-discipline until you organize your mind and keep it clear of all disturbing influences. Every principle of this philosophy must function through your mind, and self-discipline, which keeps your mind orderly, is the controlling factor in this process of becoming successful.

The following are five facts worth remembering:

1. Thoughts, ideas, and imaginations are things.

2. Our choices create our outcomes in life.

3. What we think about we become.

4. A positive mental attitude is the right mental attitude in all circumstances.

5. Our mind can only entertain one thought and/or emotion at a time.

These simple, yet powerful statements can change your life. By putting these ideas into positive daily action, a "ho-hum" mundane existence can blossom into something miraculous. Just as the butterfly transitions from the earthbound caterpillar and takes to the air, so too can this miraculous metamorphosis occur in your life.

The pattern of existence seems to indicate that first one grows roots and then wings. As your wings begin to bud, expand, and prepare you for flight, why not work to better understand the aerodynamics of your invisible self?

👈 Questions to Consider

- How committed are you to becoming the master, the ruler of your fate, your destiny?

- What is your most negative habit? What is your most positive habit? Why do you allow negativity to enter your life?

- Have you closed the door tightly on your past? Or are you lingering in the threshold?

- Are you moving forward toward your life's purpose? If not, why not?

CHAPTER 4

PURPOSE IS PERSONAL POWER

Definiteness of purpose is the foundation of all personal power.

ONCE YOU have intensified your desire to achieve a certain goal, the next step is to crystallize your desire into a definite purpose. I analyzed more than 35,000 people from all walks of life and discovered a startling fact—only two out of every 100 individuals had a defined purpose. Unsurprisingly, these two were the ones who were succeeding, while the others had drifted into mediocrity.

What distinguishes a definite major purpose from a desire?

A desire is an impulse of energy and emotion that stimulates your mind to action and activates the law of attraction to begin sending opportunities and resources in your direction.

A definite major purpose is a desire that has acquired concrete form and substance, has been located firmly in time, and has had a price tag attached. In other words, it is a commitment to put forth specific actions, according to definite plans, to add value in tangible ways, by an established deadline, so that an individual can attain a specific object or achievement to which they have laid claim.

No one ever achieved anything worth achieving without a defined purpose.

This commitment must be made in writing, for the act of writing it down signals to your subconscious mind that you have resolved to achieve your specific aim, and it recruits your subconscious mind to assist you in your efforts.

We first create the objective toward which we are striving, through the imaginative faculty of the mind, then transfer an outline of this objective to paper by writing out a definite statement of it in the nature of a definite chief aim. By daily reference to this written statement, the idea or thing aimed for is taken up by the conscious mind and handed over to the subconscious mind, which, in turn, directs the energies of the body to transform the desire to material form. Once you create your definite major purpose, you begin to operate in a state of mind conducive to achieving exactly what you desire.

It is helpful to think about a definite major purpose as being like a photograph. Those familiar with taking pictures know that there are three things needed for a good photograph: focus, proper timing, and light. If you do not attend to these three things, you will likely get a blurry picture, or at the very least, an unclear, unsatisfactory one.

The subconscious mind is like the sensitive plate of a camera and when you put on that plate a wishy-washy, indefinite picture of what you want, you may be sure you will get a blurred result. For this reason, you must put on the plate of your mind a clear picture of exactly what you want, when you want it, and what you will give in return for it.

Decide what your definite major purpose in life will be. Take your desire, in all its vivid imagery and sensory richness, and cement it into a written promise to yourself and the universe. Identify:

1. Exactly what you want (specific amount of money, specific position, particular type of thriving business, specific flourishing relationship, etc.).

2. The exact service or object you will provide in exchange for your major purpose (remember, you cannot get something for nothing).

3. The definite date you will attain your major purpose. It is crucial that you write this formula on a piece of paper or in a notebook, sign it, memorize it, and repeat it aloud at least three times a day, fully believing in your ability to achieve your major purpose.

On the same piece of paper, write a definite plan for attaining the object of your desire. Describe in detail exactly why you will believe you will accomplish your purpose, the deadlines by which you will complete each phase or element of the plan, and what you intend to give in return for your progress.

Be careful not to ask for something that is not beneficial to others, for nature, according to the law of compensation, will return payment to each individual according to what they have contributed. If you injure others in your pursuit of success, you will reap damages in return.

Moreover, be wary of including abstract or overly general elements in your definite major purpose. If your aim in life is vague, your achievements will also be vague, and it might well be added, very meager.

I know the importance of definiteness from firsthand experience. In 1919, after the end of World War I, I decided to reexamine my written document outlining my definite chief aim, and where it read, "I will earn $10,000 in 1919," I crossed it out and wrote "$100,000." I had determined to publish and edit the *Golden Rule Magazine* and knew I needed at least that much money to do so.

Immediately after editing the amount, a man came to my office from Texas and invited me to the Texas oil fields to see the men who were becoming overnight millionaires. As my visit neared the end, the man offered to employ me for a year for $100,000—to be paid at the end of the one-year term. The contract specified that if I quit before the year was over, I would not get a dime. Despite my high performance, the man was so demanding that I was forced to resign and returned to Chicago without one cent of the money promised.

From this experience, I learned that my definite chief aim was not specific enough. I should have written, "I will earn *and receive* $100,000 during the year of 1919." By including those additional two words "and receive," I would have written the need for payment into my consciousness and contract. I would have then been able to take the contract to my lawyer to ensure that I was paid for my efforts.

HOW TO APPLY DEFINITENESS OF PURPOSE

The following steps are beneficial when defining your definite purpose:

FIRST: Write a clear statement of your major purpose, sign it, and memorize it. Make sure to include:

- Exactly what you want
- What exactly you will give in return for it
- The definite date by which you will attain it
- Why you have established this as your purpose

SECOND: Repeat it at least once a day in the form of a prayer or affirmation. Make sure that you are praying in a spirit of gratitude for what you already have, because begging and complaining do not invite the positive collaboration of Infinite Intelligence. When you are grateful for the riches already within your possession, more will be added to you.

THIRD: Discipline your mind to be definite in everything you want. If you practice definiteness in the small things, then it will be easier to be definite about the large things.

FOURTH: Write out a clear, definite outline of the plan or plans to achieve the object of your purpose, and give each element of the plan a date when it must be completed. For each stage of the plan, clearly define what you intend to give in exchange for your progress. Remember, you can never get something for nothing—and if you do, it won't stay with you for long.

By applying definiteness of purpose, you will condition your mind to complete the actions necessary to attain exactly what you want. This conditioning requires you to cultivate a deep and enduring capacity for belief.

All prayer is answered within the mind, which is why you have to use language that your subconscious mind and Infinite Intelligence understand: the language of faith. Belief translates the written or spoken language you use to articulate your definite major purpose into the language of thought, a language of pure imaginative essences—where there is no gap between a word and the reality it represents.

Condition your mind to generate thought in a state of definiteness and belief, and you will refine your thought impulses to become definite thoughts and, eventually, powerful thought habits.

Definiteness is also the greatest protection you can offer your mind from the aimlessness that will derail you from accomplishing your major purpose. If you want to rise above the 98 percent who lack definiteness and can never find lasting success, you must take possession of your mind and control your thoughts so that you avoid procrastination, indefiniteness, and indecision.

Establish for yourself a mental rule that you will produce only active, definite thoughts that are grounded in belief and directed toward your chief aim, and you will become more attuned to the opportunities that surround you. You will feel your intuition expanding, but what it really will be is your sixth sense—the creative imagination—becoming more receptive to the thought impulses in your environment that align with your definite major purpose.

Your dominating desires can be crystallized into their physical equivalents through definiteness of purpose backed by definiteness of plans.

The sixth sense helps you process these thought impulses and use them to refine your definite plans for attaining your chief aim. You will discover that this process can be greatly aided—or diminished—by the nature of your emotions, which is why the next chapter turns to guidelines for controlling the emotions with which you energize your thoughts.

Now, though, let's look at how Sara Blakely imagined it and achieved it!

> SPANX founder Sara Blakely was getting ready for a party when she realized she didn't have the right undergarment to provide a smooth look under white pants. Armed with scissors and sheer genius, she cut the feet off her control top pantyhose and the SPANX revolution began! With a focus on solving wardrobe woes, the SPANX brand has secured its place in women's hearts and in pop-culture with daily mentions from CNN to SNL.
>
> In March 2012, founder Sara was named the world's youngest, self-made female billionaire by *Forbes Magazine* and one of *TIME's* 100 Most Influential People. Headquartered in Atlanta, GA, and opening retail shops across the United States, SPANX can now be found worldwide in more than 50 countries. ...SPANX shapes the world by focusing on our mission: To help women feel great about themselves and their potential.
>
> Sara Blakely states, "At Spanx, philanthropy is part of our culture. I believe in sharing the opportunity to give back directly with the people who have helped me earn the right to do so in the first place. We have a rotating philanthropy board made up

of employees. Each board is allocated a portion of the company's profits to give away. They volunteer their time to research and determine who receives the money. Employees get to make surprise visits to organizations with checks in hand and witness the tears first hand. As a company we have created a program called Leg-UP that features other female entrepreneur's products for free in our catalog. We have also built homes for families together, sent women to college, funded entrepreneurial programs in girls' schools, joined in a dance flash mob to stop violence against women, and even rendered the queen of talk, Oprah (and our accountants at the time), speechless when we donated $1 million to her Leadership Academy for girls in South Africa.

"At this stage in my life most of my time remains dedicated to growing the business. My hope is that my continued investment in Spanx will pay even greater dividends to help women. I have been setting aside profits since the start of Spanx with the goal that when the time comes I will have an amazing opportunity to help women in an even bigger way. That is part of the reason I'm making this pledge now. Setting aside the money in my foundation is only part of the preparation, learning the most effective way to give, is the other."[3]

☞ Questions to Consider ☜

- Write a clear statement of your definite major purpose, sign it, and memorize it. Make sure to include:
    - Exactly what you want
    - What exactly you will give in return for it
    - The definite date you will attain it
    - Why you have established this as your purpose

Carry this statement with you, or place it in a prominent place in your home, and repeat it to yourself at least three times a day in a state of full faith in your ability to achieve it.

- Do you agree that all prayer is answered within the mind, which is why you have to use language that your subconscious mind and Infinite Intelligence understand: the language of faith?

---

3. "SPANX, Our Story"; https://www.spanx.com/saras-world; accessed February 26, 2020.

- Identify three areas of your life, or three activities, in which you need to be more definite (procrastinate less, be more decisive and engaged, and approach it with a clear sense of how it connects with your definite major purpose). Will you make a plan for becoming more definite in these three areas?

CHAPTER 5

ENGAGING YOUR EMOTIONS

The creative faculty of the mind is set into action entirely by emotions—not by cold reason.

NOW THAT YOU have identified your definite major purpose and conditioned your mind to operate in a state conducive to its attainment, you must raise the frequency of your thought impulses so that they have more force and impact—on your subconscious mind, on Infinite Intelligence, and on other individuals. The way to stimulate your thought impulses to vibrate at a faster, more effective rate is to apply constructive emotions to them.

Stimulate your imaginative thought impulses to vibrate at a faster, more effective rate by applying constructive emotions.

Your subconscious mind is your "inner audience"—it's most influenced by emotionalized thought impulses. Of the subconscious mind, you must speak its language, or it will not heed your call. It understands best the language of emotion or feeling. Emotions are like yeast in a loaf of bread, because they constitute the *action* element, which transforms thought impulses from the passive to the active state.

Not until thought impulses have been activated by strong emotion will they induce the subconscious mind to begin translating your desire into its material equivalent. The subconscious mind is more susceptible to influence by impulses of thought mixed with feeling or emotion, than by those originating solely in the reasoning portion of the mind. In fact, there is much evidence to support the theory, that *only* emotionalized thoughts have any *action* influence upon the subconscious mind.

Strong emotions not only recruit the subconscious mind to transmute your desires into reality, but they also stimulate the creative imagination into action. As mentioned previously, your sixth sense, the *creative imagination,* is the faculty of the mind through which hunches and inspiration are received.

When the conscious mind is vibrating at an exceedingly rapid rate, as through the presence of strong emotion, the creative imagination begins receiving thought impulses from the ether, both from Infinite Intelligence and from others' minds, and processes them to generate new plans for attaining your definite chief aim. Emotions, then, are responsible for opening a direct line of communication between the finite human and the Infinite (universal intelligence), which are both a required for creativity and necessary to conceive practical plans of action.

Because both the subconscious mind and the creative imagination are heavily influenced by thought impulses mixed with emotion, it is important to familiarize yourself with the more important ones and to learn to distinguish between constructive and destructive emotions.

There are seven major positive emotions and seven major negative emotions. Unfortunately, we do not have to do any work to have negative emotions infiltrate our thought impulses—that occurs automatically, as passive thoughts are subject to contamination by negative emotions. The positive emotions, on the other hand, are not automatically injected into our thought impulses. They must be added to them intentionally through the principle of autosuggestion.

POSITIVE EMOTIONS

First, let's review the major positive and negative emotions, and then we'll explore how to cultivate positive emotions and suppress negative ones. The seven major positive emotions:

1. Desire
2. Faith
3. Love
4. Sex
5. Enthusiasm
6. Romance
7. Hope

The Emotion of Desire

Desire is the primary motivating force behind your definite major purpose. It is the intense yearning for a specific aim, experienced in the mind in rich sensory detail. Back of all achievement, back of all self-control, is that magic something called *desire!*

The Emotion of Faith

Faith is the belief in one's ability to attain a desired end. It is a requisite for success because it sets in motion actual forces by transforming the vibration of thought into a spiritual vibration. Once the subconscious mind translates the thought vibration into its spiritual equivalent, it can transmit the vibration to Infinite Intelligence, as through prayer. Faith begins with definiteness of purpose functioning in a mind that has been prepared for it by the development of a positive mental attitude. It attains its greatest scope of power by *physical action* directed toward the attainment of a definite purpose. You can voluntarily cultivate the emotion of faith by repeatedly feeding your subconscious mind affirmations of belief, by expressing gratitude for the riches already in your possession, and by taking action on your definite chief aim.

The Emotion of Love

Love is a stabilizing emotion constructive actions. When expressed in a healthy form—that is, not in a way that brings pain to the individual—it provides sanity, balance, and reason. Love is the emotion serving as a safety valve, insuring balance, poise, and constructive effort. This emotion takes various forms: familial love, or love for parents or children;

romantic love, or love for one's sweetheart; the love that exists in true friendship; and love for inanimate and nonhuman objects, such as nature. All shapes and shades of love can inspire reformation, or the desire to better oneself through the pursuit of one's definite chief aim. The emotion of love also provides a balancing function for the emotion of sex, combining with romance to form a mental trifecta that generates purpose, poise, and accuracy of judgment. Caution: love can also induce individuals to succumb to drifting, that state of aimlessness that leads to mediocrity and failure. For this reason, love must never be allowed to take over the mind in such a way that the individual neglects to develop definiteness.

The Emotion of Sex

Faith and desire are psychical emotions that work on the subconscious mind in spiritual ways. The emotion of sex, on the other hand, is a biological force: it harnesses the body's physical drives to energize the mind's creative impulses. The emotion of sex is the most powerful of all the stimuli that move people into action. However, it is also one of the most volatile emotions: its energy must be redirected from carnal ends and converted into other, more productive channels. In other words, you must take thoughts of physical sex expression and invest them in thoughts of a different, higher nature. When you channel sexual urges into thoughts pertaining to your definite major purpose, you acquire the following benefits: a super power for action, an irresistible force (personal magnetism or charisma) that draws others into your service, and unmatched creative powers. This latter capability is particularly important: anywhere creative genius is present, the transmuted emotion of sex must be present, as the emotion of sex contains the secret of creative ability.

The Emotion of Enthusiasm

Like the emotion of sex, enthusiasm is an emotion that provokes the individual to action and stimulates the mind's creative faculties. It ensures that you will remain motivated in your pursuit of success, as it keeps your body and mind recharged and invested in your purpose and plans. This emotion is also contagious: it enables you to gain the cooperation of others in your endeavor—for who can remained unmoved by someone who is incredibly passionate about their goals *and* is taking action on them? In addition, enthusiasm influences others to become more active agents in their own lives. This is because enthusiasm supports the principle of suggestion, whereby your words and your acts and even your state of mind influence others. With the aid of enthusiasm, your personality will become more dynamic, as your words and actions will be colored with invigorating energy, and you will develop the habit of concentration of endeavor. Those looking to cultivate the emotion of enthusiasm should engage in work or activities that provide them with the satisfaction of meaningful labor and service.

The Emotion of Romance

The emotion of romance collaborates with the emotions of sex and love to infuse your words and actions with calmness of purpose, amorous desire, and constructive effort. There should be an element of romance to all that we do. As with the emotion of sex, our romantic feelings can be channeled to other endeavors to generate excitement and interest. There is nothing sweeter than fresh romance: it energizes our movements, speeds up the vibrations of our thoughts, and develops keenness of focus on the object of our desire. Once we stimulate the mind with the emotion of romance, we can develop courage, willpower, and persistence that are unknown to us at other times.

The Emotion of Hope

Hope keeps your focus fixed on the future—on the certainty that you will attain your definite chief aim. It is not to be confused with a hazy desire, a passive wish for fate to bring you what you seek. The constructive emotion of hope is a state of mind that is at peace because it is sure of future achievement. It is the largest contributor toward happiness, which lies always in the future and never in the past.

> Hope is the largest contributor toward happiness, which lies always in the future and never in the past.

NEGATIVE EMOTIONS

The seven major negative emotions:

1. Fear
2. Jealousy
3. Hatred
4. Revenge
5. Greed
6. Superstition
7. Anger

In the great stream of life, there are two currents that flow in opposite directions. The side of the stream that carries an individual to success and fulfillment is made of positive emotions. The other side, which brings an individual to poverty, failure, and unhappiness, is comprised of negative emotions. It is the responsibility of every individual to learn to control their emotions so that their "chemistry of the mind" does not become toxic to them through the presence of harmful combinations of emotions. The presence of any one or more of the destructive emotions in the human mind, through the chemistry of the mind, sets up a poison which may destroy one's sense of justice and fairness.

The presence of a single negative thought in your conscious mind is sufficient to destroy all changes of constructive aid from your subconscious mind. Fear is the source from which all negative emotions flow. For this reason, it is helpful to catalog the six basic fears in order to discern which are influencing your thought impulses:

1. Fear of Poverty

2. Fear of Criticism

3. Fear of Ill Health

4. Fear of Loss of Love

5. Fear of Old Age

6. Fear of Death

We look more closely at these in the next chapter.

Search out the source of your negative emotions, determining which fear, or combination of fears, they are rooted in. Then use the faculty of willpower to discourage the presence of any negative emotion in your mind. The mind creates thought habits out of the dominating thoughts that are fed to it. Control of the mind, through the power of will, is not difficult. Control comes from persistence, and habit. The secret of control lies in understanding the process of transmutation. When any negative emotion presents itself in your mind, it can be transmuted into a positive, or constructive emotion, by the simple procedure of changing your thoughts.

Develop an awareness of the emotions that are characterizing your thoughts. Actively cultivate positive emotions and transform negative emotions into positive ones. Form the habit of applying and using the positive emotions! Eventually, they will dominate your mind so completely, that the negatives *cannot enter it*. Most people dissipate their emotions by sowing them in the wrong fields. Avoid this trap by investing your emotions in creating and carrying out plans to achieve your definite major purpose.

MASTER MIND ALLIANCE

Beyond emotions, there are constructive mental stimuli that can temporarily, or even permanently, increase the rate of your vibrations of thought. These include music and the master mind alliance—a group of like-minded individuals set on achieving a certain goal. Listening to music can stimulate your thought impulses to such a high frequency that your creative imagination becomes more alert, more receptive to vibrations from Infinite Intelligence and others' minds. Similarly, by forming and participating regularly in a master mind group, you can heighten your thought vibrations.

In a master mind alliance, the thought impulses of the different members, all directed toward the same aim, are jointly raised to a level unattainable by a single mind. This is the psychic dimension of the master mind, the "third mind. No two minds ever come together without, thereby, creating a third, invisible, intangible force that may be likened to a third mind. The spiritual units of energy generated from the master mind alliance allow the members to generate thought impulses that have more power over the subconscious mind and more magnetic force for attracting opportunities and answers.

> **The world is ruled and the destiny of civilization is established by the human emotions.**

Thought impulses characterized by desire and definiteness have power. Thought impulses backed by desire, refined by definiteness, and magnetized by a combination of the constructive emotions can create physical change in the world. When thought impulses attain a higher level of vibration through stimulation by the constructive emotions, they put an individual in direct connection with Infinite Intelligence, heighten the creative faculties, and influence others to offer their assistance. Remember: The world is ruled and the destiny of civilization is established by the human emotions. *Learn to harness them for your success!*

☞ Questions to Consider ☜

For each of the positive emotions, use your imagination to identify a means for channeling it toward the pursuit of your definite major purpose.

The Emotion of Desire: What images and experiences create longing in your heart and mind? Imagine the feeling of intense yearning and apply this emotion to your chief desire.

The Emotion of Faith: What images and experiences (prayer, yoga, spiritual retreats, etc.) generate spiritual connection and/or supreme belief in yourself, a spiritual entity, or others? Imagine the feeling of complete trust and confidence resulting from connection with yourself, others, or a superior being and apply this emotion to your chief desire.

The Emotion of Love: What images and experiences create the feeling of deep affection that solidifies bonds between yourself and something outside of yourself? Imagine all types of love—familial, romantic, friendship, love of nonhuman objects—and experiment with connecting the feelings of love generated by these different relationship types to your chief desire.

The Emotion of Sex: What thoughts and experiences create sexual excitement, interest, and energy for you? Imagine accomplishing your major purpose, channeling the emotional energy toward it.

The Emotion of Enthusiasm: What images and experiences get you excited and motivated to take action? Imagine the feeling of impassioned eagerness and apply this emotion to your chief desire.

The Emotion of Romance: What images and experiences create romantic feelings for you? Imagine the emotion of romance and apply it to your definite major purpose.

The Emotion of Hope: What images and experiences make you hopeful that a desire will come to fruition? Imagine feelings of certainty that you will accomplish your major purpose and stimulate the thought of your chief desire with the expectation that it will become reality.

- Which negative emotion, or combination of negative emotions, is operating in your mind presently?
- Which of the six basic fears is responsible for each of your negative emotions?

Make a plan for transforming your negative emotions into positive ones.

CHAPTER 6

FACING AND OVERCOMING FEAR

ALL THOUGHT impulses originate from one of two sources: fear or desire. Both are emotions related to wanting, but they work in opposite directions. You desire what you *do* want; you fear what you *don't* want. Because fear and desire are contrasting emotions, it is counterproductive to have both operating in your mind at the same time. They will vie for dominance until one succeeds at amplifying itself from an impulse of emotion to a full-fledged state of mind.

Fear is mental quicksand. The negative thoughts that originally gave fear a foothold enlarge and reproduce until the mind is completely paralyzed and unable to form constructive, positive thoughts. Indecision, procrastination, worry, greed—these are just some of the damaging effects of operating from a position of fear. It is impossible to attain your chief aim in life if your thoughts are bogged down by fear. You will always be moving backward, never forward; always missing opportunities, never recognizing or acting on them; always succumbing to failure, never seeing temporary defeat as an invitation to a newer, better plan.

FEAR OF POVERTY

The fear of poverty inspires poverty consciousness, leading to thought habits characterized by indifference, indecision, doubt, worry, and overcautiousness.

FEAR OF CRITICISM

The fear of criticism destroys your creative faculties, freedom of thought, and initiative. The fear of criticism is particularly prominent in individuals whose parents were highly critical of them in childhood, causing them to develop an inferiority complex. It leads to thought habits characterized by self-consciousness, meekness, indecision, inferiority, extravagance, lack of initiative, and lack of ambition.

FEAR OF ILL HEALTH

The fear of ill health is closely related to the fear of old age and the fear of death: all three come from humans fearing what happens after they die. It often produces the very symptoms it dreads because disease can begin as a negative thought impulse. It leads to thought habits characterized by an addiction to health fads, hypochondria, self-indulgence, and intemperance.

FEAR OF LOVE LOSS

The fear of loss of love arises when people worry about infidelity or abandonment by their romantic partner. It leads to thought habits characterized by jealousy, fault-finding, injudiciousness with money, and adultery.

FEAR OF OLD AGE

The fear of old age results from concern about the afterlife, poverty in old age, and loss of freedom of thought and activity resulting from the aging process. It leads to thought habits characterized by immaturity, nostalgia, inferiority, and a lack of imagination.

FEAR OF DEATH

The fear of death similarly results from concern about the afterlife. It leads to thoughts characterized by inaction, a fear of poverty, and religious fanaticism.

So, the first step in controlling your thoughts is to rid your mind of fear and its offspring: doubt, unbelief, greed, envy, jealousy, and superstition. You cannot productively focus on both what you desire and what you do not desire simultaneously. Autosuggestion—the principle where your dominant, repeated thoughts seek a physical form—does not discriminate between negative thoughts and positive thoughts. If strong fears are present in your mind, your subconscious will work to translate them into material reality—just as it would constructive desires.

Replace fear with faith!

Begin now to change the chemistry of your brain by conditioning your mind to operate in a state of belief. To replace fear with faith, you must cultivate a positive mental attitude, because faith resides only in a mind characterized by positivity. A positive mental attitude is like a fertile field in which you can plant the seeds of your definite major purpose. Cultivate this by focusing on how you can add value to others' lives.

If you frame your desires in a context of service, they will be firmly embedded in a powerful emotional network that will repel fears, incite action, and invite the cooperation of Infinite Intelligence, the great storehouse of universal energy that some call "God" and others call "Nature." The following formula helps you cleanse your mind of lingering fears and complaints and begin anew with the seeds of faith.

Once you clear your mind of negativity and create a state of mind characterized by belief and self-confidence, you can identify the desire that will become your definite major purpose. No definite major purpose will have power unless backed by desire. A definite chief aim would be meaningless unless based upon a deeply seated, strong desire for the object of the chief aim. Many people wish for many things, but a wish is not the equivalent of a strong desire, and therefore wishes are of little or no value unless they are crystallized into the more definite form of desire.

Dispense with any self-imposed limitations and consider now what is the one thing you want more than anything else in life. You have already emptied your mind of doubts and fears, so you are not allowing concerns about money, education, time, or anything else to stand in your way of determining your primary desire. *Use your imagination—don't hold back.*

Think in big terms, but choose something that is within the range of what can be expected of someone with your capabilities, age, and intelligence. Questions to consider include the following: What is the pinnacle of success for you? If you could accomplish one thing in life, what would it be? Is it a relationship? A business? A position? An amount of money? A charitable act?

No one can select your dominating desire for you, but once you select it for yourself, it becomes your definite chief aim and occupies the spotlight of your mind until it is satisfied by transformation into reality—unless you permit it to be pushed aside by conflicting desires.

THE FOUNDATION OF DESIRE

I wish to be of service to others as I journey through life. Living in fear makes an enjoyable life journey impossible. Establishing a foundation of desire makes fear flee.

I have adopted the following creed as a guide to follow in dealing with my fellow human beings—and overcoming every fear in the process:

- To train myself so that never, under any circumstances, will I find fault with any person, no matter how much I may disagree or how inferior his or her work may be, as long as I know the person is sincerely trying to do their best.

- To respect my country, my profession, and myself. To be honest and fair with others, as I expect them to be honest and fair with me. To be a loyal citizen of my country. To speak of it with praise, and act always as a worthy custodian of its good name. To be a person whose name carries weight wherever it goes.

- To base my expectations of reward on a solid foundation of service rendered. To be willing to pay the price of success in honest effort. To look upon my work as an opportunity to be seized with joy and made the most of, and not as a painful drudgery to be reluctantly endured.

- To remember that success lies within myself—in my own brain. To expect difficulties and to force my way through them.

- To avoid procrastination in all its forms, and never, under any circumstances, put off until tomorrow any duty that should be performed today.

- Finally, to take a good grip on the joys of life, so I may be courteous to everyone, faithful to friends, and true to God.

Note that your dominating desire must not violate the rights of others, and it should be something that you truly want—because once you set the wheels of this success system in action, the principles will deliver you the object you have determined to create or acquire, regardless of whether it is good or pleasant to you. In order to plant in your mind the seed of a desire that is constructive, make the creed the foundation of your code of ethics and the bedrock of all your efforts to succeed.

Once you have named your primary desire, the next step is to work to develop it from a hazy wish to a strong impulse of thought to, eventually, a driving passion. For although desires begin as a flash of inspiration, they must be fertilized with belief and nurtured to become a dominating obsession that transcends everything else. Over time, a strong desire properly cultivated will become a fact—a certainty that your definite chief aim is already within your possession; you merely have to find a way to claim it.

A strong desire is one that you can experience as real. Use all of your senses—including your imagination—to give your desire multi-dimensionality. The language of thought is not restricted to the symbols and sounds that make up our spoken and written language, it is based more on sensory impressions and concepts than anything else.

If you cannot find the right words to describe your primary desire fully, use other means: Draw it. Find its music. Determine its texture, taste, and sound. Use all the means at your disposal to imagine and then create a detailed image, or clip, of your desire. Paint a picture of what you want that is so definite and clear that none—particularly yourself—can mistake it.

Continue to use your imagination to experience your primary desire in all its sensory richness on a daily basis. By holding it at the forefront of your mind, you will ensure that your actions align with your intentions. What is more, you will activate the law of attraction, a universal force that acts upon a constant, deeply seated, strong desire to attract its physical counterpart, or at least the means of securing it.

This law stimulates your mind to recognize objects, people, and opportunities within your environment that have bearing on your dominating desire. For example, if you desire a particular position, suddenly you will take more notice of training opportunities that will qualify you for the role you seek. You will find yourself drawn to individuals who have some connection with the desired organization or field, enabling you to build your network and gain access to more opportunities related to your chief aim.

Desire is a magnetic force. When its elements are not guided by a strong magnetic field, like that of your mind, they will lose their alignment and become weakened, and fears may reappear. But when in the presence of a strong guiding force, the impulses that create desire regain their unified directionality and acquire strength.

Desire is also a form of energy. When it is stored and not put into action, it remains latent—as potential energy—unless it is transformed into negative emotions, fears or thoughts, or diminished through aimless thoughts and actions. But when activated, its kinetic energy causes transformations in the physical environment, creating or securing your chief aim.

AN OPEN MIND

An open mind is a free mind—and a mind filled with fears holds you captive, in bondage.

Those whose minds are closed because of fears don't experience new ideas, exciting concepts, and interesting people. Fears lock a door that enslaves their own mentality. Fear and intolerance is a two-edged scythe that on its backswing cuts off opportunities and lines of communication. When you open your mind, you give your imagination freedom to act for you.

> Open your mind and give your imagination freedom.

It's hard to realize now that less than six decades ago there were people who laughed at the Wright Brothers' experiments at flight. And barely three decades ago, Lindbergh could scarcely find backers for his trans-Atlantic flight. Then, no one laughed when mentioning going to the moon. It was the scoffers held in scorn.

A closed mind is a sign of a static personality. It lets progress pass it by and hence can never take advantage of the opportunities progress offers.

Only if you have an open mind can you grasp the full impact of the first rule of the science of success—*whatever the mind can conceive and believe, the mind can achieve.*

It would be well for you to take stock of yourself. Are you among those who say "I can" and "It will be done"—or do you fall in the group that says, "Nobody can," at the very moment somebody else is accomplishing it?

An open mind requires faith—in yourself, in others, and faith in the Creator who laid out a pattern of progress for you and His universe. The days of superstition are gone. But the shadow of prejudice is as dark as ever. You can come out into the light by closely examining your own personality. Do you make decisions based on reason and logic rather than on emotion and preconceived ideas? Do you listen closely, attentively, and thoughtfully to the other people's arguments? Do you seek facts rather than hearsay and rumor?

The human mentality withers unless in constant contact with the stimulating influence of fresh thought. Our nation's enemies in their brainwashing technique, know that the quickest way to break a person's will is to isolate his mind, cut him off from books, newspapers, radio, and other normal channels of intellectual communication.

Under such circumstances, the intellect dies for lack of nourishment. Only the strongest will and the purest faith can save it.

Is it possible that you have imprisoned your mind in a social and cultural concentration camp? Have you subjected yourself to a brainwashing of your own making, isolating you from ideas that could lead to success? If so, it's time to sweep aside the bars of prejudice that imprison your intellect. Open your mind and set it free!

> Have you imprisoned your mind in a social and cultural concentration camp?

I was asked to speak at a college graduation and I told the audience, "There is a great lesson for you young people in all this. It's simply this: no matter how optimistic and hopeful my words sound today, no matter how I let my imagination roam, no matter how glowingly I describe the future, I cannot possibly hope to draw a full picture of the glorious achievements mankind will accomplish during the next thirty-five years!"

AIN'T SEEN NOTHIN' YET!

At this point I'm reminded of the taxicab driver in Washington, DC, who drove a tourist past the Government Archives Building. On the building there is carved a motto that reads:

"What is Past is Prologue."

"What does the motto mean?" the visitor asked.

"Well," said the driver, "it means you ain't seen nothing yet!"

The things you are destined to see during your lifetime, the glorious accomplishments in which you will take part, defy description!

Many years ago, I propounded a theory that has since been repeated so often that it now sounds like a platitude. The fact remains, however, that the truth of my statement is being proved every day. What is that statement? Simply this:

Whatever the mind can conceive and believe, the mind can achieve!

Your future—your attainments and achievements—will be limited only by the limits of your imagination!

There is no doubt that you will experience disappointments and temporary setbacks. And there's no doubt either that collective tragedy—possibly in the form of war or depression—will afflict your generation as it did those that went before you.

But here I can offer you another truth from the science of personal achievement that was my pleasure to formulate during the past fifty years: every adversity carries with it the seed of an equivalent benefit.

> **Every adversity carries with it the seed of an equivalent benefit.**

It's up to you, however, to find this seed, nurture it, and bring it to full growth and fruition. No one can do this for you. Each of us, with the help of our Almighty Creator, creates our own destiny. And by like token, each of us must find those hidden benefits that He grants us in moments of adversity.

Let me repeat once more those two statements that I think form the pillars upon which you may, with faith, build the structure of a successful life. The first is, *whatever the mind of man can conceive believe, the mind can achieve.* Second, *every adversity carries with it the seed of an equivalent benefit.*

If you master these two concepts, you will have taken two giant strides toward achieving happiness—within a fearless life.

☞ Questions to Consider ☜

- What is the pinnacle of success for you?
- If you could accomplish one thing in life, what would it be? A relationship? Business? Position? Amount of money? Charitable act?
- Have you subjected yourself to a brainwashing of your own making, isolating you from ideas that could lead to success?

CHAPTER 7

IMAGINING IDEALS

Imagination: The habit of arranging old ideas into new combinations, and the alertness of mind to quickly recognize circumstances to be avoided, or opportunities to be embraced.

O NE WAY a person can use creative imagination is in the purposeful planning for peace. Everywhere we are bombarded with signs and symbols of aggravation, dissension, and indicators of aggression that ultimately lead to unrest, chaos, and war. What makes it so, and how can one person ultimately make a difference?

Driving to work yesterday, I actively looked for the usual signs of spring that herald the season of renewal in northwest Indiana. Returning robins, budding pussywillows, longer days, and greening grass are all present for the viewing. These harbingers come naturally and when they return, an almost audible sigh of relief is heard indicating that spring is once again in the works.

But yesterday I noticed man-made beauty too. Some yards had flower beds displaying yellow daffodils that added beauty to residences. Some neighbors were collecting litter that accumulated over the winter and are tidying up their spots on the planet. Dead leaves are being raked up and bagged for disposal. As the outdoors is spruced up, evidence of interior cleaning occurs too. This caused me to wonder—imagining ideals!

What would happen if everyone did the following, or at least attempted some of the following:

- Construct and maintain a flower bed with seasonal blooms that passersby could enjoy, sort of like eye candy for the soul. Wouldn't some people slow down and admire the festival of colors? Friendly cooperation could occur as one neighbor learns from another. Growing the best morning glories, marigolds, zinnias, four-o'clocks, roses, hollyhocks, petunias, pansies, moonflowers, etc., could replace our attraction to the gore of the daily news. Seeds can be cultivated and shared over a cup of coffee or tea. Just think of the beauty and the small cost of creating such wonder! What imaginative construct could you begin with just a shovel, soil, seeds, and self? Go for it. Make someone's day this way!

- In Ireland, communities are recognized for being "Tidy Towns." As you enter a town, a large congratulatory sign is displayed indicating the award and the year it was received. When seen, this sends a message to all that the town respects the environment and the community. People tend not to litter because the town openly displays the value of having clean and welcoming surroundings.

- Driving to work I can count by blocks the roadkill that litters the streets in various forms of decomposition along the highways I travel. Cats, dogs, deer, raccoons, possums, skunks, fowl, rats, and even turtles are daily reminders of life's untidy consequences. Probably on my daily 30-mile, one-way commute, I can count without trying 30-40 carcasses along my path. Not too pleasant of a sight. Why not tidy up, or have town management offer this service for a fee? This view of our environment negatively colors our perception of the world.

- Similarly, the litter of trash including paper, plastic bags, cans, clothes, and every form and frame of garbage can be found along the country roads as well as suburban and city streets. Imagining a landscape free of litter is an ideal worth considering and taking action to make it so.

- If each of us took care of our allotted space on this planet by making an attempt to beautify it, wouldn't the world take on a better appearance little by little? Ralph Waldo Emerson states that the "Earth laughs in flowers." Gandhi says, "Be the change that you want to see in the world." "Each one teach one" is a good way to begin. It doesn't take much creative imagination to shove a spade into the earth and plant some seeds. But it does take the Creator to manifest the outpouring of new life. Are you ready to be a harbinger of spring and beauty? Plant for today, bloom for tomorrow, and decide right now to make a positive statement for improvement, not perfection, in the here and now.

> **Plant for today, bloom for tomorrow, and decide right now to make a positive statement.**

THE EXTRA MILE

Along those same idealistic lines, going the extra mile leads to the development of a positive, pleasing mental attitude, which is among the more important traits of a pleasing personality and lifestyle.

And going the extra mile—doing more than you are expected or paid to do—also tends to develop a keen, alert imagination because it is a habit that keeps you continuously seeking new and more efficient ways of rendering useful service. I don't think that I have ever engaged in delivering a lecture or writing a book that I didn't learn something during that effort that I hadn't learned before.

Incidentally, I learned something about public speaking last week. I didn't know about it until I received reports back from those who heard the speech. Those reports remind me that we can never become so perfect or so good or so successful that we aren't agreeable to learning. As long as your mind is open, as long as you are willing to learn, as long as you remain green, you'll grow. But the moment you become ripe, the next step is to become rotten.

PERSONAL INITIATIVE

Going the extra mile tends to develop a keen, alert imagination. A keen, alert imagination causes you to constantly look for new ways of rendering service. Also, it develops the important factor of personal initiative, without which no one may attain any position above mediocrity and without which no one may acquire economic freedom. If you don't develop the habit of personal initiative—doing what you ought to be doing without somebody telling you to do it or going along with you to see that you do it—you'll never get very far in life.

This business of going the extra mile and making it your business to take pleasure out of going the extra mile certainly does develop personal initiative. It causes you to get joy out of acting on your own initiative. And incidentally, that's the one thing that nature intended every human being should do. Nature gave you the unquestionable right of power over your own mind and expected that you would solve your problems and, to an extent, work out your earthly destiny by the operation of your mind. But it always depends on your use of personal initiative—something you have to do for yourself; you can't assign it to somebody else.

Of course, there are a lot of people in the world who depend on others to do their thinking for them, but people who are willing to do that reject the greatest prerogative that's been given to them by the Creator—the right to act upon, and use, and direct, and control their own minds.

Personal initiative is the most outstanding trait of the typical successful American citizen, and this is a nation literally built upon personal initiative. If it had not been for the personal initiative of those 56 brave men who signed the most marvelous document ever known to man—the Declaration of Independence—if it had not been for their personal initiative in crafting and signing it, we wouldn't be free agents today.

We wouldn't be able to go out and about in these United States of America doing the things we want to do, saying the things we want to say, as we can today. It's been the personal initiative of great industrialists, great railroad builders, and great financiers that has made this the richest and the most desirable country on the face of this earth—and has given us the highest standard of living ever known to mankind.

Men and women of initiative are willing to go on their own, take their losses, make their failures, enjoy their successes, and take the full responsibility for their acts—those are the kind of people who get ahead in this world, not those who are looking for public relief or somebody to take care of them in their old age.

If feeling insecure, there is one institution I can recommend where you have absolute security, but I don't think you would want to go there. That's the penitentiary. You can get in there very easily, and you don't need to worry, as your troubles are over for the rest of your life.

I prefer to meet life on my own terms, to imagine my ideals coming true, to meet life's conditions as they are on my own initiative, and to trust my knowledge of these marvelous principles of nature to get me to where I want to go in life and to get me there with the least amount of resistance.

And next, going the extra mile definitely serves to develop self-reliance. When looking over the reports after I give a speech, three factors are emphasized more than all the others: enthusiasm; self-confidence; and poise. Almost everyone grades me "perfect." Now, where do you suppose I got that poise and that self-reliance and that enthusiasm? I got it by putting into everything I do the best that I have in active physical effort, in mental effort, and in spiritual effort—giving the best that I have, expecting that the best would come back to me.

And lo and behold, the time did come when not only the best came back to me, but everything that my mind could conceive that I wanted, or desired, or could use was available to me.

And next, going the extra mile serves also to build the confidence of others in your integrity and general ability. I don't know of any one thing that will raise you in the minds of other people more than for them to observe, as you go about your duties in your professional life—your business, or your job, or your work, or whatever it may be—as you go about that responsibility, that you are giving the best you have. You're not watching clocks; you're not griping, you're not complaining; and you're not expecting the world owes you a living. I like people who believe that the world owes them only one thing—the privilege of giving to the world the finest that they have to give.

IF I HAD A MILLION DOLLARS

The following story proves the truth of that old saying, "Where there's a will, there's a way." It was told to me by a beloved

IMAGINING IDEALS

educator and clergyman Frank W. Gunsaulus, who began his preaching career in the stockyards area of Chicago.

While Dr. Gunsaulus was going through college, he observed many defects in our educational system. Defects that he believed he could correct, if he were the head of a college. He made up his mind to organize a new college where he could carry out his ideas, without being handicapped by orthodox methods of education.

He needed one million dollars to begin the project, but where could he get such a large a sum of money? That was the question absorbing most of this ambitious young preacher's thoughts. But he couldn't seem to make any progress.

Every night he took that thought to bed with him. He got up with it in the morning. He took it with him everywhere he went. He turned it over and over in his mind until it became his consuming obsession.

Being a philosopher as well as a preacher, Dr. Gunsaulus recognized, as do all who succeed in life, that definiteness of purpose is the starting point from which one must begin. He recognized, too, that definiteness of purpose takes on life and power when backed by a burning desire to translate that purpose into its material equivalent.

He knew all these great truths, yet he did not know where or how to lay his hands on a million dollars. The normal thing would have been to give up and quit, saying, "Ah, well, my idea is a good one, but I can't do anything with it because I can't raise the million dollars." That is exactly what the majority of people would have said, but not what Dr. Gunsaulus said. What he said and did are so important that I'll let him speak for himself:

> "One Saturday afternoon I sat in my room thinking of ways and means of raising the money to carry out my plans. For nearly two years I had been thinking, but I had done nothing but think. The time had come for action!
>
> "I made up my mind, then and there, that I would get the necessary million dollars within a week. How? I was not concerned about that. The main thing of importance was the decision to get the money within a specified time. I want to tell you that the moment I reached a definite decision to get the money within a specified time, a strange feeling of assurance came over me such as I had never before experienced. Something inside me seemed to say, 'Why didn't you reach that decision a long time ago? The money was waiting for you all the time!'
>
> "Things began to happen in a hurry. I called the newspapers and announced I would preach a sermon the following morning entitled 'What I Would Do If I Had a Million Dollars.'
>
> "I went to work on the sermon immediately, but I must tell you frankly that the task was not difficult,

because I had been preparing that sermon for almost two years.

"Long before midnight I had finished writing the sermon. I went to bed and slept with a feeling of confidence, for I could see myself already in possession of the million dollars.

"Next morning I arose early, went into the bathroom, read the sermon, then knelt on my knees and asked that my sermon might come to the attention of someone who would supply the needed money.

"While I was praying I again had that feeling of assurance that the money would be forthcoming. In my excitement, I walked out without my sermon and did not discover the oversight until I was in my pulpit and about ready to begin delivering it.

"It was too late to go back for my notes, and what a blessing that I couldn't go back! Instead, my own subconscious mind yielded the material I needed. When I arose to begin my sermon, I closed my eyes and spoke, with all my heart and soul, of my dreams. I not only talked to my audience, but I fancy I talked also to God. I told what I would do with a million dollars if that amount were placed in my hands. I described the plan I had in mind for organizing a great educational institution, where young people would learn to do practical things and at the same time develop their minds.

"When I had finished and sat down, a man slowly arose from his seat, about three rows from the rear, and made his way toward the pulpit. I wondered what he was going to do. He came into the pulpit, extended his hand, and said, 'Reverend, I liked your sermon. I believe you can do everything you said you would, if you had a million dollars. To prove that I believe in you and your sermon, if you will come to my office tomorrow morning, I will give you the million dollars. My name is Philip D. Armour.'"

Young Gunsaulus went to Mr. Armour's office and the million dollars was presented to him. With that money he founded the Armour Institute of Technology, now known as Illinois Institute of Technology.

The million dollars that launched the Armour Institute came as a result of an idea. Behind the idea was a desire that young Gunsaulus had been nursing in his mind for almost two years.

Observe this important fact: he got the money within 36 hours after he reached a definite decision in his own mind to get it—and decided upon a definite plan for getting it!

There was nothing new or unique about young Gunsaulus' vaguely thinking about a million dollars and weakly hoping for it. Others have had similar thoughts. But there was something very unique and different about the decision he reached on that memorable Saturday, when he put vagueness into the background and definitely said, "I will get that money within a week!"

The principle through which Dr. Gunsaulus got his million dollars is still alive. It is available to you. This universal law is as workable today as it was when the young preacher made use of it so successfully.

👉 Questions to Consider

- How long have you been imagining an ideal?
- What is your ideal imagination?
- When will you reach a definite decision—and decide on a definite plan to get it?

CHAPTER 8

MOTIVATIONS AND MACHINATIONS

Be motivated by love and see how quickly this emotion is given wings for action through faith... which becomes a labor of love.

THOUGHTS REQUIRE both emotion and logic to entice the subconscious mind to translate your definite chief aim into material reality. Therefore, in addition to applying a mixture of the emotions detailed in a previous chapter, it is important to adopt a combination of compelling motives, or reasons for action, to place behind your definite major purpose.

In other words, you need to embed your desire within a logical structure that gives it purpose and momentum—a momentum that will be attractive both to the subconscious mind and to positive workings, which solidify behaviors into habits and habits into rhythms.

All voluntary physical action is inspired by one or more of the nine basic motives. If you don't back your purpose with a proper number of these motives, you are not going to be invested in carrying out that major purpose after you adopt it. You will not have a burning desire to initiate and complete actions toward achieving your definite purpose unless you have a motive that sets you on fire. The more of these motives you recruit for your aims, the more likely you will be to accomplish your goals.

Unless you have a motive(s) that sets you on fire, you will not initiate and complete actions toward achieving your definite purpose.

Consider the following catalog of the nine basic motives and determine which motive or combination of motives best serves your purposes by providing your desire with a solid, logical framework in which it can gain strength.

Note that the last two motives on the list are negative in nature, and although they can inspire action, it is usually toward a destructive end. It is best to ground your actions in positive motives; otherwise, you will undercut yourself by moving in the wrong direction or acting in ways that take value away from others, rather than adding it to them.

NINE BASIC MOTIVES

Desire for Love

The greatest of all motives is love—and not just physical attraction, but love in a broader sense. We feel love for our family, for our romantic partners, for our friends, for our country and communities. We feel love for both human and nonhuman creatures, animate and inanimate things. Love is the opposite of jealousy; it is rooted in contentment and gratitude. We love people and things because we appreciate their unique attributes and recognize the value that they add to our lives—and the value we bring to them as well. When we are motivated by our love for someone or something, it becomes incredibly easy to take the necessary steps to accomplish our aim because we see the value it will bring to our relationship. Let a person be motivated by Love and see how quickly this emotion is given wings for action through Faith. The action becomes a labor of love. Our actions become more purposeful because they are service oriented, and we reap more joy from our labors because we recognize that our efforts will strengthen our love.

Desire for Sex

This desire gives the means of perpetuating life. When motivated by the desire to reproduce, we situate our actions and goals within a generational framework. Our behaviors gain increased significance because they are driven by a desire for legacy—for ensuring not only the continuation of the species and the family, the macro and the micro, but also the ability of posterity to enjoy the fruits of our labors. In addition to biological and generational considerations, the desire for sex is also anchored in the pleasure drive. By redirecting your desire toward the accomplishment of your major purpose, you generate energy and incentive for achievement. And when you combine the motives of sex and love, you compound your motivation and gain enormous power for action.

Desire for Material Wealth or Money

This desire inspires us to develop our ingenuity and discover ways to build wealth. It is not rooted in a fear of poverty but rather in money consciousness—the awareness that we have all the tools we need at our disposal to increase our income and grow our net worth. When we are motivated by the desire for material wealth or money, our tendency to procrastinate diminishes, as it becomes easier not only to complete our responsibilities and tasks, but also to go the extra mile in our work. We seek out opportunities to expand our value and provide more service in our efforts to achieve our definite major purpose, rather than viewing each step along the way as a box that has to be checked off.

Desire for Self-Preservation

The desire for self-preservation is a relatively self-explanatory motivation. We all desire to live, and to live fully. Any time we can frame our desire in the context of its fulfillment of our basic human needs—food, shelter, clothing, belonging; the emotional and physical essentials for survival—we have a primal motivation to take action.

Desire for Freedom of Body and Mind

The majority of people desire wealth so they can obtain freedom of body and mind. In general, human beings do not like to be beholden to other individuals. The more money we have, the more we are able to control our circumstances. When we direct our thoughts toward achieving freedom of body and mind and enjoying the satisfaction that comes from true self-sufficiency, we discover an almost spiritual urge to persist in our efforts. This motive is particularly compelling for individuals who seek to get out of debt, build wealth, start their own business, or gain independence in some other form.

Desire for Self-Expression

As human beings, we tend not only to desire freedom of body and mind, but also the freedom to express ourselves—particularly in a way that enables us to gain public recognition. This motive is the desire to attract the attention of others and to impress them favorably. When we believe our actions will result in the recognition of our special talents, gifts, and abilities, or will permit us to excel over others, we are less likely to experience burnout in our success journey.

Desire for Life After Death

The desire for life after death is the motive on which all religious activity is based. When our definite chief aim is rooted in a spiritual purpose or calling, we find the willpower to accomplish feats that would otherwise prove too difficult. Our weaknesses lose their power over us, as we gain the self-discipline and courage necessary to take consistent action on our goals. We believe ourselves to be supported by a higher being, so our efforts are magnified beyond our own abilities. Moreover, we believe our purpose to have eternal significance, which makes it that much easier to stay committed to achieving our definite chief aim.

Desire for Revenge

The desire for revenge is the first of two negative motives. When we are motivated by the desire to strike back—to take justice into our own hands and right a wrong that we believe we experienced—we might find the incentive to take action. However, the actions will surely send us in the wrong direction. The law of compensation dictates that our actions will be returned to us in kind, which means that any actions we take in a spirit of revenge will generate negative returns in our lives. Even if these negative consequences do not directly result from the actions we take in seeking revenge, they are certain to come at some point. Plans based on unjust or immoral motives may bring temporary success, but enduring success must take into consideration…time. It is therefore crucial that we assess our motivation to ensure it is free of the desire to get revenge on someone. Even if, for example, we desire success to rise above someone who has wronged us, we are sure to find ourselves on the negative side of hypnotic rhythm, the negative manifestation that renders permanent destructive thought habits and behaviors and guarantee our ultimate failure.

Emotion of Fear

As with the desire for revenge, the emotion of fear inspires action that is undercut by destructive thought impulses. All six of the basic fears cause individuals to act, not in faith or service to others, but out of doubt, worry, and distrust. Such emotions debilitate the mind's reasoning faculty, preventing it from identifying productive means of accomplishing your aims and encouraging it to take actions in the wrong direction. Fear, as a motive, will keep you in mental, emotional, spiritual, and financial poverty throughout your life, because it prevents you from using your personal initiative to create positive change in your life.

Fear, as a motive, prevents you from using your personal initiative to create positive change in your life.

Place behind your definite major purpose one or more of these positive motives, and you will find the resistances of life fade into nothingness. Emotionalize your thought impulses, giving them strength and intensity, and then provide them with structure and direction by situating them within a compelling motive structure.

When your thought impulses are directly linked to emotion and logic, you will discover the following benefits: Your mind will be prepared for action. Joy will crown your every effort. Self-discipline will become as natural as breathing. You will identify the secrets to influencing others, and you will strengthen your human relationships. For motives dictate not only the direction and ultimate success of your actions, but also the nature of your character.

This brings me to the heart of this chapter on motivations and machinations. I must tell you what I consider to be the five essential characteristics or traits that lead to success in life, which are found in the formula for faith.

Motives dictate not only the direction and ultimate success of your actions, but also the nature of your character.

FORMULA FOR FAITH

FIRST: I know that I have the ability to achieve what I want in life. I commit to performing the necessary actions, continuously and persistently, regardless of obstacles that come my way.

SECOND: I recognize that the dominating thoughts of my mind will reproduce themselves in outward action and eventually translate themselves into physical reality. Therefore, I will concentrate my thoughts daily on the type of person I wish to become—positive, benevolent, enthusiastic, decisive, prompt, and steadfast.

THIRD: I realize that any desire I persistently hold in my mind will eventually seek expression in material form, so I will dedicate time each day to feeding my mind thoughts of belief in my abilities, including the ease with which I can translate my desires into reality.

FOURTH: I recognize that desire, in and of itself, does not guarantee my individual success. Anyone can have a desire; what separates truly successful individuals from the rest of the population is their ability to evolve their desire into a consuming passion and their willingness to take action on it. With that in mind, I commit to using the principles outlined in this book to cultivate my imaginative thought impulses into definite thought habits and, eventually, rhythms of thinking that have greater force in attracting their aims. I will not dishonor my deepest desires by allowing them to remain in wish or hope form; I will render them active through their intentional development and implementation.

FIFTH: I fully realize that lasting success can never be built upon injustice or untruth, so I will refrain from engaging in any activity that threatens the rights or livelihood of others. I will seek to provide service to all people through my efforts to achieve success, and I will focus on inviting cooperation from others, rather than subduing or surpassing them.

☞ Questions to Consider

For each of the seven positive motives, how can you rationalize your purpose according to the logic of each of these seven constructive motives?

Desire for Love

How is your definite major purpose an expression of the love you feel for your family, your romantic partner, your friends, your community, or your country? For example, how are you helping someone or something you love, and in the process strengthening that relationship, by fulfilling your purpose?

Desire for Sex

For example, how is your definite major purpose driven by your desire to build a legacy? Or how is your definite major purpose a means of experiencing the pleasure of finding an outlet for your creative energy?

Desire for Material Wealth or Money

How will your definite major purpose bring you monetary rewards such as wealth, security, and independence either now or in the future? How does it provide material advantages?

Desire for Self-Preservation

How does accomplishing your definite major purpose enable you to ensure that you will have the basic physical and emotional necessities for survival—food, shelter, clothing, and belonging?

Desire for Freedom of Body and Mind

How does attaining your chief desire provide you with control over your circumstances? How does it enable you to dictate how your time, talent, and money are spent? For example, does it give you financial security and independence so that you are not beholden to your employer? Does it free you from some other form of emotional or physical bondage?

The Desire for Self-Expression

How does actualizing your chief desire enable you to express your unique individuality and obtain recognition for your talents? What is impressive about it that is specific to your gifts, skills, and/or creative pleasures?

The Desire for Life After Death

How does accomplishing your major purpose build up treasures in the afterlife, thereby compounding its significance? Or how does it memorialize your identity on earth long after your death? For example, are you fulfilling a calling that has been placed on you by a higher being? Are you providing a service to others that blesses their lives, and thus your own, in some way?

- How is fear or the desire for revenge holding you back in your success journey? Do you find yourself beating against a wall or moving backward because you are negatively motivated?

- Will you make a plan to eliminate negative motives and replace them with one or more of the seven positive motives?

CHAPTER 9

RHYTHM OF THOUGHT

The person who thinks in terms of power, success, and opulence, **sets up a rhythm which attracts these desirable possessions.** The person who thinks in terms of misery, failure, defeat, discouragement, and poverty attracts these undesirable influences. This explains why both success and failure are the result of habit. Habit establishes one's **rhythm of thought,** and that rhythm attracts the object of one's dominating thoughts.

AFTER STRENGTHENING your imaginative thought impulses by magnetizing them with constructive emotions, and after providing them with form and function through the adoption of a compelling motive structure, it is time to transform your thoughts into thought habits.

A thought attains the level of habit through the forces of concentration and repetition. As habits increase in strength, they become a powerful rhythm. Any impulse of thought the mind repeats over and over through habit forms an organized rhythm. This organized rhythm makes it easier to generate new thoughts that align with your definite major purpose, and it attracts thought impulses and resources from external sources that will increase the ease with which you achieve your goals. Through the power of habit, our thoughts gain the force necessary to translate our desires into physical reality.

Through the power of habit, your thoughts gain the force necessary to translate your desires into physical reality.

As thoughts become habits, they harmonize to form a structured pattern—a pattern that takes on its own nature. Individual habits gain power through their networked relation to other habits that align with their purpose. In order to take advantage of this habitual rhythm, you must voluntarily put in your mind a thought that you want to keep (concentration) and continue bringing it back into your mind (repetition).

CONCENTRATION

Concentration, otherwise known as controlled attention, is the act of focusing the mind on a given desire until ways and means for its realization have been worked out and successfully put into operation. Concentration is also the ability to think as you wish to think, the ability to control your thoughts and direct them to a definite end, and the ability to organize your knowledge into a plan of action that is sound and workable.

At its core, concentration is about possessing singularity of focus—both in your thoughts and your actions. You cannot do or think a dozen different things at a single time. Trying to do that makes you a jack-of-all-trades—someone trying to think and do too many things at once and accordingly lives a scattered, mediocre life. Rather than allowing your thoughts to be pulled in different directions, you must focus them on a singular aim.

When we become skilled at holding definite thoughts in our mind, we activate the subconscious mind and the imagination to identify a practical plan for translating our desire into reality. This, in turn, makes it easier to create positive behavioral habits. It is nearly impossible to create long-term change in our actions without first changing the nature of our thoughts.

TRANSFORM THOUGHTS INTO THOUGHT HABITS

To transform your thoughts into thought habits, organize your thoughts by drawing a very clear and definite mental picture of what you wish to acquire or of the person you wish to be, and then concentrate on that picture until you transform it into a physical reality. Blend together all the different subjects and ideas and imaginations that create the perfect picture of your primary aim, and hold these thoughts in your mind until the subconscious mind solidifies them into habits, which attract a positive workings rhythm.

The opposite of concentration is drifting, which occurs when individuals allow passive, negative, directionless thoughts to operate in their mind. These disorganized thoughts translate into habits of aimlessness and procrastination, which create a rhythm that ushers individuals toward failure.

The mind wants to operate according to the path of least resistance, and the natural path of least resistance is fear and indecision. *Whenever you are not intentionally placing constructive thoughts in your mind through concentration, your mind will begin to drift, and you will develop thought habits that work against your success.*

Eventually, hypnotic rhythm will take over and fix these directionless thoughts in a potent rhythm. If the same thought is held in the mind, or left there by neglect, for a certain length of time, nature takes it over, through the rhythm of habit, and makes it permanent. Once hypnotic rhythm has taken hold of your destructive thought habits, it becomes incredibly difficult to extricate yourself from the negative flow of energy. Therefore, it is crucial to foster constructive thoughts and dismantle negative impulses before they consolidate into a rhythm.

Get rid of negative impulses before they consolidate into a rhythm.

The corrective for drifting is definiteness and decisiveness. Ensure you are forming complete, purposeful thoughts out of which positive thought habits and behavioral habits can grow.

Be definite in everything you do and never leave unfinished thoughts in the mind. Form the habit of reaching definite decisions on all subjects!

Acquire the habit of intentionally placing positive thoughts in your mind, and make sure to follow every thought to its logical end. Avoid hazy thoughts or ones that are not future oriented. Wishy-washy thoughts, as well as thoughts that are rooted in the past, are subject to the manipulations of negative external influences, causing your destructive thoughts to strengthen and multiply. You can avoid this trap through concentration, which enables you to cultivate concrete positive thoughts that become habits of thinking.

HABITS OF THINKING

A habit is formed through repetition. It creates a mental path whose grooves become deeper and wider as our thoughts and actions continue to travel over that same path. These grooves increase the ease with which we engage in the same thoughts and behaviors, and they make it difficult to think and act in different directions. Our habits grow out of our environment. Remember:

> The human mind draws the material out of which thought is created from the surrounding environment, and habit crystallizes this thought

into a permanent fixture and stores it away in the subconscious mind where it becomes a vital part of our personality, which silently influences our actions, forms our prejudices and our biases, and controls our opinions.

Because it is difficult for our mind to rise above our environment, we need to be attentive to the nature of our surroundings. Our thoughts will harmonize with our environment, so we must place ourselves in situations that are conducive for forming and maintaining constructive thought habits. For example, if you surround yourself with people who are poverty conscious, your mind will extract the fear and indecision from the thought impulses in your surroundings and create thought habits that will keep you in poverty.

Similarly, if you place yourself in a context in which independence of thought, decisiveness, and self-discipline are valued and practiced, your thought habits will become characterized by definiteness and initiative. As we do the same things and think the same thoughts over and over again, our habits begin to resemble a cement block that cannot be broken. This is when the habit turns into a permanent rhythm of thought or behavior.

If your thought habits are not currently supporting your success, you can form new mental pathways that attract the positive workings of rhythm. The best way to remove old habits that are not serving you is by creating new ones. As you form new habits, the old mental pathways will lose their sharpness and will begin to dissipate over time. I've crafted a guide for forming desirable habits. Once you replace destructive habits with constructive ones, you will no longer have to stand behind your desire and push it—beyond this point, the desire will stand back of you and push you on to achievement.

Our thoughts must acquire strength and consistency in order to fully harness the powers of the subconscious mind and Infinite Intelligence to translate them into reality. Like any language, the language of thought must be developed beyond concepts and words into complete sentences. The grammar and syntax of imaginative thought language are concentration and repetition, which enable us to fill out our thoughts so that they become a pattern—a pattern that transforms into the story of our success. *Are you ready to write your story with more powerful language?*

Take a moment right now to concentrate on your primary desire using the details identified in the last question. Fix in your mind a vision that blends together all of these elements, and then work to refine it by completing any details that are missing or hazy. Ensure this vision is oriented toward the future.

While holding this vision in your conscious mind, direct your subconscious mind to identify the best plan for actualizing your desire. Use your imagination! Take notes on the ideas that are generated through this exercise. Repeat this activity until a definite, practical plan becomes apparent to you.

HOW TO FORM A DESIRABLE HABIT RHYTHM

FIRST: At the beginning of the formation of a new habit, put force and enthusiasm into your expression. Remember that you are taking the first steps toward making the new mental path and that it is much harder at first than it will be later. Make the path as clear and as deep as you can at the beginning so you can readily see it the next time you wish to follow it.

SECOND: Keep your attention firmly concentrated on the new path building, and keep your mind away from the old paths, lest you incline toward them. Forget all about the old paths, and concern yourself only with the new ones you are specifically building.

THIRD: Travel over your newly made paths as often as possible. Make opportunities for doing so, without waiting for them to arise through luck or chance. The more frequently you go over the new paths, the sooner will they become well-worn and easily traveled. Create plans for passing over these new habit-rhythm paths at the very start.

FOURTH: Be sure that you have mapped out the right path as your definite chief aim, and then go ahead without fear and without allowing yourself to doubt. Place your hand on the plow, and don't look back. Select your goal, then make good, deep, wide mental paths leading straight to it.

👉 Questions to Consider 👈

- How have your thoughts been characterized by indecision, aimlessness, and/or negativity? How have your thoughts been pulled in different directions so that your mental processes are bogged down by competing impulses?
- How can you replace these thoughts characterized by drifting with more constructive thoughts?
- Can you create and identify all that is necessary to paint a complete picture of your definite goal and its achievement?

CHAPTER 10

FREESTYLE FREEDOMS

No one can be entirely free spiritually, mentally, physically, and economically without learning the art of accurate thinking.

U P TO THIS POINT, all of the strategies that have been described are a form of offense—how we can progress in our success journey by enhancing our use of imagination. But because the mind is subject to external influences, it is equally important to bolster our lines of defense around our thoughts. The way to protect our subconscious mind from negative outside influences is through accurate thinking.

Protect your subconscious mind from negative outside influences through accurate thinking.

To safeguard your thoughts from destructive influences, you must engage in three mental processes:

- First, separate facts from mere information.
- Second, distinguish between important and unimportant facts—relevant and irrelevant ones.
- Third, become adept at organizing, classifying, and using the sound, relevant facts you retain in your mind.

To be sure that your thoughts are accurate, subject them to the control of the will and the faculty of reason. Most so-called thinking is the work of the emotions without the guiding influence of self-discipline, without relationship to either the power of the will or the faculty of reason. That is why the majority of thoughts produced are impotent at best and destructive at worst—they are undercut by the faulty logic that results from negative and uncontrolled emotions.

> **Accurate thinking is characterized by freedom from dogma, bias, or the need for approval from others and infused with emotions of faith, courage, hope, and definiteness of purpose.**

Inaccurate thoughts result from ignorance, superstition, intolerance, and fear. Accurate thinking, in contrast, is characterized by freedom from dogma, bias, or the need for approval from others, and it is also infused with the emotions of faith, courage, hope, and definiteness of purpose.

Whenever the accurate thinker gathers information from external sources—or receives unsolicited information from others—he or she scrutinizes both the content of the message and the character of the source to determine its veracity. The accurate thinker puts aside all negative emotions and judges the message and its sender objectively.

The eyes of the accurate thinker sees facts—not the delusions of prejudice, hate, and envy. In contrast to the majority of people today, who prefer to remain in their own echo chambers so that their preconceived notions can be reinforced by everyone with whom they interact, the accurate thinker seeks out a multitude of perspectives and assesses each one with openness and controlled emotion.

Spiritual and economic freedom, the two highest aims of which human beings are capable, are available only through the proper use of the mind.

ACCURATE THINKING

Accurate thinkers can quickly discern false or misleading information when it is tinged with slander or negative emotions. They do not accept without question public opinion, which tends to search out reasons for vilifying original thinkers. Rather than relying on the noise of the media or the whispers of gossip, accurate thinkers perform extensive research on information presented to them, consults with a master mind group, and leverages their own logical faculties to render an informed, impartial decision on a given matter. They allow no room for snap judgments—only scientific and accurate ones.

Accurate thinkers have no opinions and make no decisions that have not been submitted to and passed on by the faculties of the will and the reason. They use their emotions to *inspire the creation of ideas through their imagination*, but refine their ideas through will and reason before final acceptance. This is self-discipline of the highest order. Accurate thinkers maintain a firm standard of evaluation for all information and allow only facts to influence their thought processes.

Once the accurate thinker has distinguished facts from information, the thinker must discern what constitutes an important and a relevant fact. An important and relevant fact is any fact that you can use, without interfering with the rights of others, in the attainment of your major purpose. All other facts, as far as you are concerned, are superfluous and of minor importance at most.

More basically, all thoughts you can use in the attainment of your definite chief aim are important and relevant; all that you cannot use are unimportant and irrelevant. One of the biggest differences between people who are successful and those who do not achieve their goals is the latter group who muddles their thoughts with ideas that are not useful for attaining their definite major purpose. Concentration, as described in the previous chapter, enables you to focus your thoughts on the ideas that align with your primary desire and filter out those that are irrelevant to your aims.

ACCURATE THINKERS ENGAGE IMAGINATION

Finally, after separating fact from information and selecting only the most relevant facts to keep fixed in their mind, accurate thinkers become adept at organizing, classifying, and using the chosen thoughts. Engaging the faculty of the synthetic imagination—the portion of the mind that rearranges existing knowledge to produce new combinations—accurate thinkers order and reorder facts until they generate a practical plan of action. In this way, accurate thinking goes beyond defense, participating in the mind's creative function as it transforms ideas into their most profitable, constructive form.

These three mental processes described are all a matter of controlling your thoughts, which is entirely within your power. Although these processes occur within the mind, there are two additional elements that can increase your ability to engage in accurate thinking. The first of these is your physical health. If you are not taking care of your body, it clouds your mind and prevents accurate thinking. In particular, it is important to consume healthy foods that support your cognitive processes.

Foods that are too rich or that cause indigestion can slow down your reasoning faculty and generate negative emotions that obstruct rational thought.

The second external element that impacts your ability to think accurately is your relationships. If you are married, the quality of your thoughts can be raised or lowered depending on the nature of your partnership. As explored in the previous chapter, your environment is the source from which the material of our thoughts is drawn. In a harmonious marital union, our minds can join together and generate higher-level thoughts. However, if our union is not harmonious, we are susceptible to inaccurate thinking and the habit of drifting.

Our other relationships, such as our friendships and work relationships, can also influence our thoughts. But aside from our marriage relationship, the most impactful relationship on our thoughts is the one with our master mind alliance. When we participate in a harmonious group of likeminded individuals who encourage independent thinking and refuse to accept failure as final, we can take advantage of the "third mind" created from the alliance: the spiritual energy generated through the affinity produces a force that increases the frequency at which every member's thoughts vibrate, enhancing their creative and logical abilities.

I offer six principles, and your comprehension of each is critical for accurate thinking. I urge to you follow these guidelines to protect your mind from negative external influences that prevent accurate thinking. After all, accurate thinking is the solution to all problems, the answer to all prayers, the source of opulence and all material possessions.

> Accurate thinking is the solution to all problems, the answer to all prayers, the source of opulence and all material possessions.

LEARN TO THINK ACCURATELY

To learn how to think accurately, you must thoroughly understand:

FIRST: Your mind can be controlled, guided, and directed to creative, constructive ends.

SECOND: Your mind can be directed to destructive ends and that it may, voluntarily, tear down and destroy unless it is with plan and deliberation controlled and directed constructively.

THIRD: Your mind has power over every cell of the body and can be made to cause every cell to do its intended work perfectly, or it may, through neglect or wrong direction, destroy the normal functionary purposes of any or all cells.

FOURTH: That all your achievement is the result of thought, the part that your physical body plays being of secondary importance, and in many instances of no importance whatsoever except as a housing place for the mind.

FIFTH: That the greatest of all achievements, whether in literature, art, finance, industry, commerce, transportation, religion, politics, or scientific discoveries, are usually the results of ideas conceived in one person's brain but actually transformed into reality by others, through the combined use of their minds and bodies.

SIXTH: The majority of all thoughts conceived in your mind are not accurate, being more in the nature of opinions or snap judgments.

Once you have mastered the art of accurate thinking, you will experience a freedom unknown to other individuals, the vast majority of whom allow the noise of the media and the naysayers to disrupt their thoughts and steal their peace of mind.

THE CRADLE OF FREEDOM AND HUMAN LIBERTY

The Creator provided that life on this earth will continue according to His plans, no matter what people may think they want, nor to what motives they may attribute the results of their personal initiative.

This is a fact well known to every psychologist, but not everyone may recognize the possibility that in back of all expressions of personal initiative is the Creator's plan to assure our mental and spiritual growth through our own endeavors.

Two facts stand out like the sun in the heavens on a clear day:

1. The United States of America has grown to be the one of the most successful nations of the world, and has become known as the "cradle of freedom and human liberty" on a scale that has made it an example for all the world to observe and emulate.

2. The most outstanding feature of the American people as a whole is their well-known habit of moving on their own personal initiative.

And it has been no mere stroke of chance that blessed Americans with these two outstanding benefits that have provided unparalleled privileges of growth and progress. The privilege of having our own resourcefulness overshadows all other privileges we enjoy—this privilege of free enterprise through which the humblest people may choose their own motives and live their own lives and accumulate riches in whatever form and quantity they desire.

In this country, the first great master mind alliance was made up of our nation's founders. From the alliance of the great minds of the thirteen original colonies comes American liberty and freedom. The alliance between the great minds of the first states of the Union created a greater variety of opportunities for the exercise of individual initiative than exists anywhere else in the world today. American "know-how" and imagination is still the greatest in the world—and don't let anyone tell you differently.

The master mind mandate evolved on a global scale during World War II. What would the world be like today if the allied nations had not formed a master mind alliance? The United States and its allies were fighting for the continuation of personal freedom, opposing another alliance determined to destroy personal freedom. For any alliance to endure, it must be based on justice and fairness for all it affects.

The United States consists of 50 states joined together in a mutual cooperative alliance based on a Constitution that was voted on and accepted by a majority of the people of all the states. America's source of riches, freedom, and power can be directly traced to that intangible something known as "spirit" in which men and women work together for the realization of a common end. When the imaginative spirit of teamwork is willing, voluntary, and free, it results in a very great and enduring power.

The American way of life is friendly teamwork. It is founded on a philosophy of freedom and opportunity for all who make contributions to its support, in proportion to each person's individual talents expressed through a friendly system of free enterprise.

The same principle of friendly, cooperative teamwork applies to success in business and your ability to sell yourself and your skills. The habit of rendering more and better service than you are immediately compensated for develops the important factor of personal initiative, without which no one may attain any position above mediocrity, and without which no one may acquire economic freedom. Personal initiative is the most outstanding trait of the typical American citizen—this is a nation literally built on personal initiative and imagination.

This principle of freedom, this most cherished privilege of self-determination, has made America the richest and freest nation on the face of the earth. We must see to it that nothing ever removes this incentive to excellence. Humankind has been endowed by the Creator with the right of choice in our thoughts, and our government has preserved and defended the privilege of exercising this God-given right. This right has made the USA "the land of the free and the home of the brave"!

Our great nation, with all of its riches and all of its freedom, is literally a product of temporary defeat, a form of defeat that awakened in the hearts of our founders the determination that led them eventually to the discovery of that "seed of an equivalent benefit" which the defeat carried.

George Washington's early military campaigns ended in the most discouraging sort of defeat. But Washington was destined to prove to the world that temporary defeat need not be accepted as failure. He accepted defeat as nothing more than an inspiration to greater and more persistent effort.

And this, my friend, is the heart of this book for you, your family, career, and even a nation—*imagining,* working, trying, failing, facing fear, overcoming, thinking, and *achieving!*

☞ Questions to Consider

- Will you be creating guidelines to distinguish between relevant and irrelevant facts when granting access to your subconscious mind?
- Can you identify three steps to improve your health that will improve your ability to think accurately?
- How can you leverage your relationships to improve the quality of your thoughts? If you are not part of a master mind group, will you form

one to take advantage of the psychical and cognitive benefits it provides?

- Is your personal initiative a dominating aspect of your personality? Do you go above and beyond what is asked of you? What difference could you make in your family life, career, and personal achievements if you used your imagination and focused on going the extra mile?

CONCLUSION

YOU NOW HAVE the tools you need to imagine it and achieve it. But having the tools is only half the journey; as with any endeavor, you must apply what you learn by developing true fluency in imagination.

The steps you take now to achieve your imaginations will determine your success. For the language of thought is the language of success: the subconscious mind and Infinite Intelligence, those two psychic forces that provide you with inspiration, refine your plans for achievement, and sustain you through the challenges that come your way, speak only in this language. Without the aid of these forces, the journey to redesigning your desires into reality will be significantly longer and more difficult.

Commit now to using your mind with more intentionality and intensity. Practice the principles outlined in this book with regularity and the support of a master mind alliance or study group, and you will develop more success in the pursuit of your chief aim and greater freedom in all areas of life.

1. Identify the burning desire that would be the pinnacle of success for you. Rid yourself of any fears that diminish the intensity of this desire, and replace these fears with faith in your ability to redesign your imaginations into reality.

2. Refine your thought impulses related to your chief desire into a definite major purpose. Remember, a definite major purpose is *a commitment to put forth specific actions, according to definite plans, to add value in tangible ways, by an established deadline, so to attain a specific object or achievement.*

3. Magnetize your definite major purpose by emotionalizing your thought impulses with the positive emotions of desire, faith, love, sex, enthusiasm, romance, and hope.

4. Back your thought impulses with logic by packaging them in a compelling motive structure using one or more of the following constructive motives: the desire for love, the desire for sex, the desire for material wealth or money, the desire for freedom of

body and mind, the desire for self-expression, and the desire for life after death.

5. Use concentration and repetition to establish a rhythm of thought into mental habits that attract the positive workings of the universal law of nature that turns habits into rhythms and gives you increased momentum on your success journey.

6. Protect your mind with accurate thinking, separating facts from mere information, distinguishing between important and unimportant facts, and effectively organizing, classifying, and using the sound, relevant facts you retain in your mind.

These six principles are the building blocks of success: desire, purpose, emotion, motive, concentration, repetition, and accuracy. When your imaginations are arranged and combined in the proper way, they form a comprehensible force that compels your subconscious and Infinite Intelligence to work in your favor to translating your dreams into material reality.

You will get the most out of what you learned in this book by putting into practice the positive mental attitude and the master mind alliance principle. This you can do (as others are doing so successfully) by forming a study club consisting of any desired number of people who are friendly and harmonious. It is recommended that the group meet regularly, as often as once each week, and should consist of reading one chapter of this book—or any Napoleon Hill book—at each meeting and discussing the contents freely by all members. Each person should take notes, writing ideas that come to mind inspired by the discussion.

Wealth and riches cannot always be measured in money!

By following this plan, you will benefit not only from the sum total of the best knowledge organized from the experiences of hundreds of successful individuals, but more important by far, you will access new sources of knowledge in your own mind as well as acquire knowledge of priceless value from others present.

Remember, riches cannot always be measured in money! Money and material things are essential for the freedom of body and mind, but there are some who will feel that the greatest of all riches can be evaluated only in terms of lasting friendships, harmonious family relationships, sympathy and understanding

CONCLUSION

between business associates, and introspective harmony that brings peace of mind measurable only in spiritual values.

Get ready to experience a changed life filled with harmony and understanding and for the accumulation of wealth in abundance!

Nevertheless, if you understand and apply the steps and adopt this philosophy to imagine it and achieve it, you will be better prepared to attract and enjoy higher estates that always have been and always will be denied to all except those who are ready for them.

Be prepared, therefore, when you expose yourself to the influence of this philosophy to experience a changed life that can help you not only to negotiate your way through life with harmony and understanding, but also prepare you for the accumulation of material riches in abundance!

ABOUT NAPOLEON HILL

Napoleon Hill
(1883-1970)

"Remember that your real wealth can be measured not by what you have—but by what you are."

NAPOLEON HILL was born in Wise County, Virginia. He began his writing career at age 13 as a "mountain reporter" for small town newspapers and went on to become America's most beloved motivational author. His work stands as a monument to individual achievement and is the cornerstone of modern motivation. His most famous work, *Think and Grow Rich,* is one of the best-selling books of all time. Hill established the Foundation as a nonprofit educational institution whose mission is to perpetuate his philosophy of leadership, self-motivation, and individual achievement.

In 1908, during a particularly down time in the U.S. economy and with no money and no work, Napoleon Hill took a job to write success stories about famous men. Although it would not provide much in the way of income, it offered Hill the opportunity to meet and profile the giants of industry and business—the first of whom was the creator of America's steel industry, multimillionaire Andrew Carnegie, who became Hill's mentor.

Carnegie was so impressed by Hill's perceptive mind that following their three-hour interview he invited Hill to spend the weekend at his estate so they could continue the discussion. During the course of the next two days, Carnegie told Hill that he believed any person could achieve greatness if they understood the philosophy of success and the steps required to achieve it. "It's a shame," he said, "that each new generation must find the way to success by trial and error, when the principles are really clear-cut."

Carnegie went on to explain his theory that this knowledge could be gained by interviewing those who had achieved greatness and then compiling the information and research into a comprehensive set of principles. He believed that it would take at least twenty years, and that the result would be "the world's first philosophy of individual achievement." He offered Hill the challenge—for no more compensation than that Carnegie would make the necessary introductions and cover travel expenses.

It took Hill twenty-nine seconds to accept Carnegie's proposal. Carnegie told him afterward that had it taken him more than sixty seconds to make the decision he would have withdrawn the offer, for "a man who cannot reach a decision promptly, once he has all the necessary facts, cannot be depended upon to carry through any decision he may make."

It was through Napoleon Hill's unwavering dedication that his book, *Think and Grow Rich,* was written and more than 80 million copies have been sold.

THANK YOU FOR READING THIS BOOK!

If you found any of the information helpful, please take a few minutes and leave a review on the bookselling platform of your choice.

BONUS GIFT!

Don't forget to sign up to try our newsletter and grab your free personal development ebook here:

soundwisdom.com/classics